Organization Info

MW01268746

Name	
Address	
Email Address	
Phone Number	
Fax Number	

Record Information

Start Date	
Book Number	
Others	

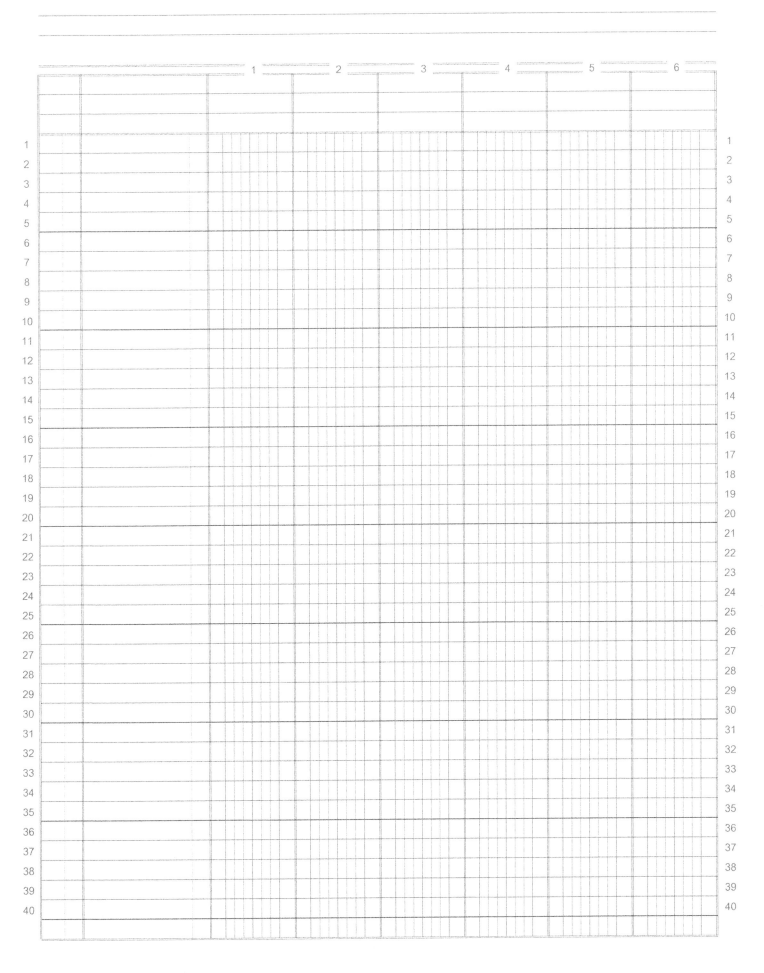

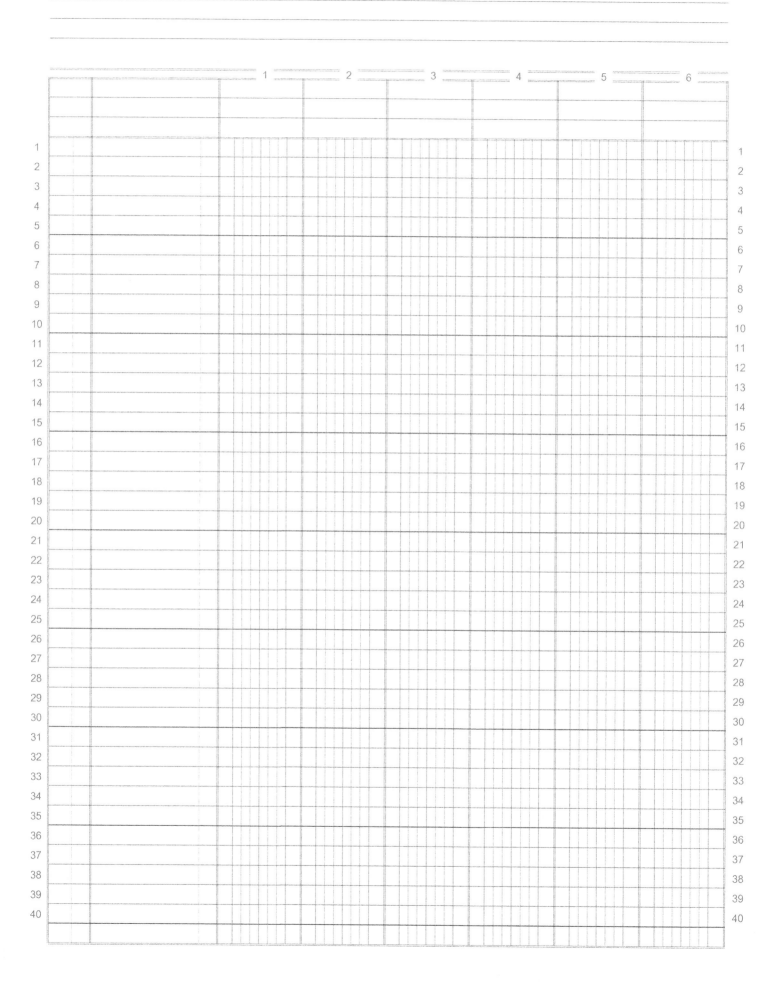

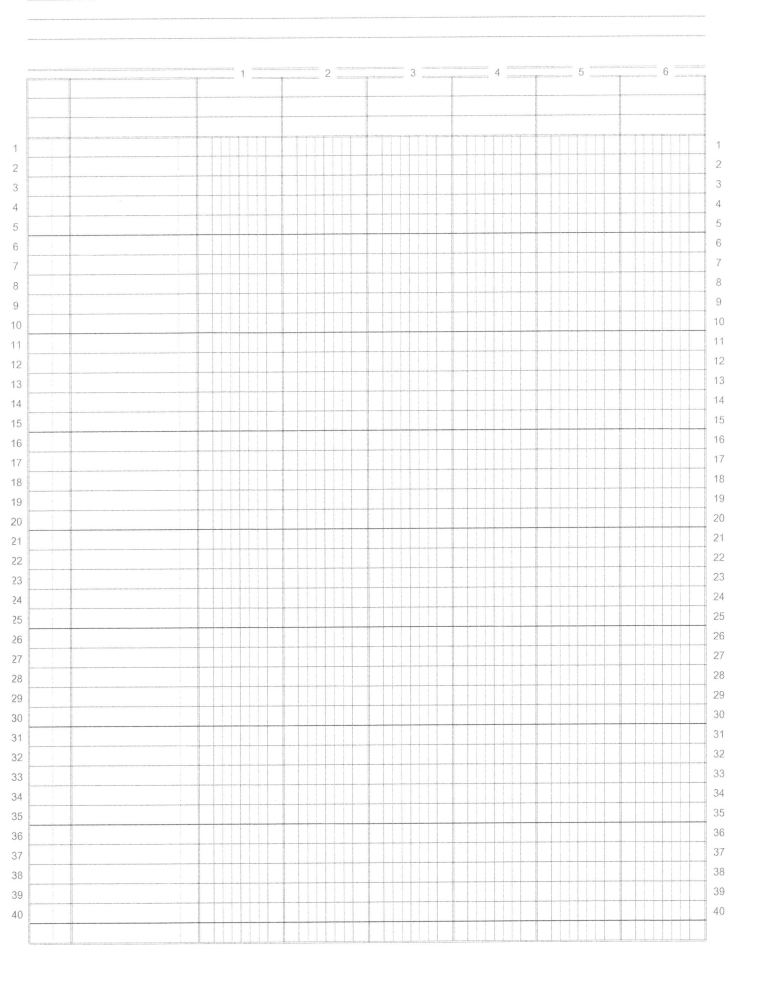

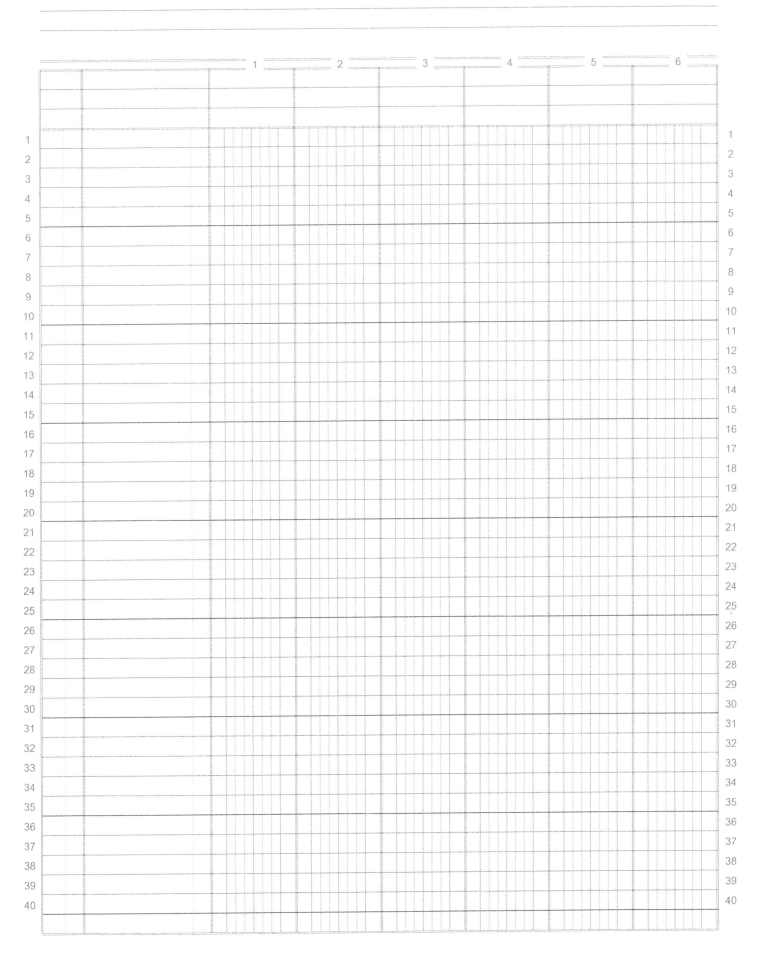

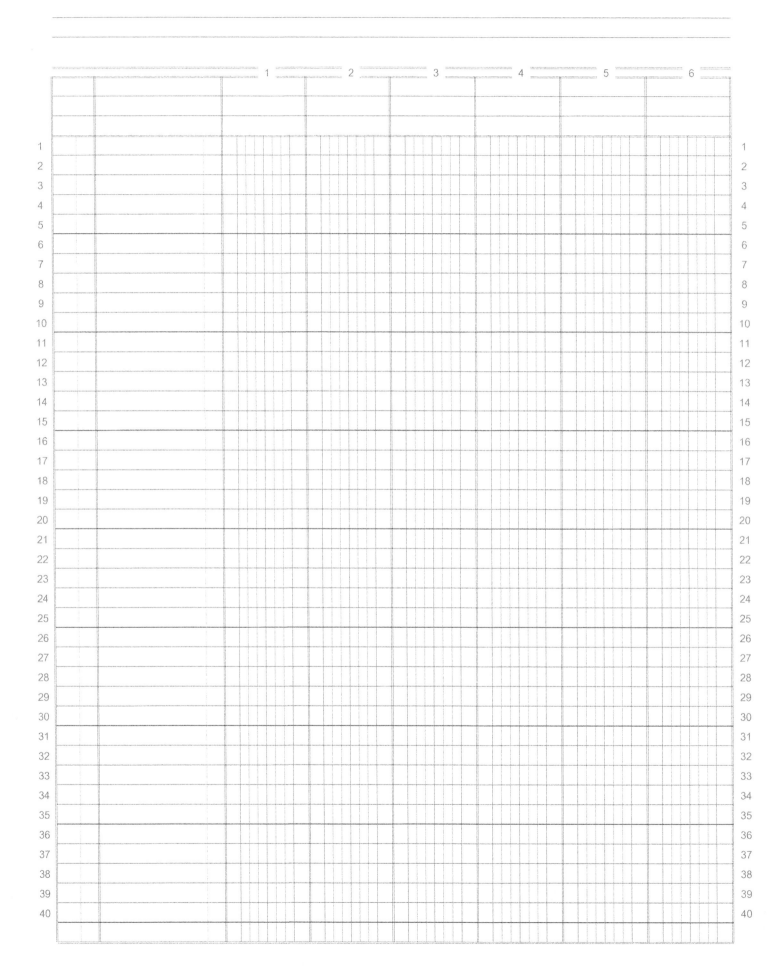

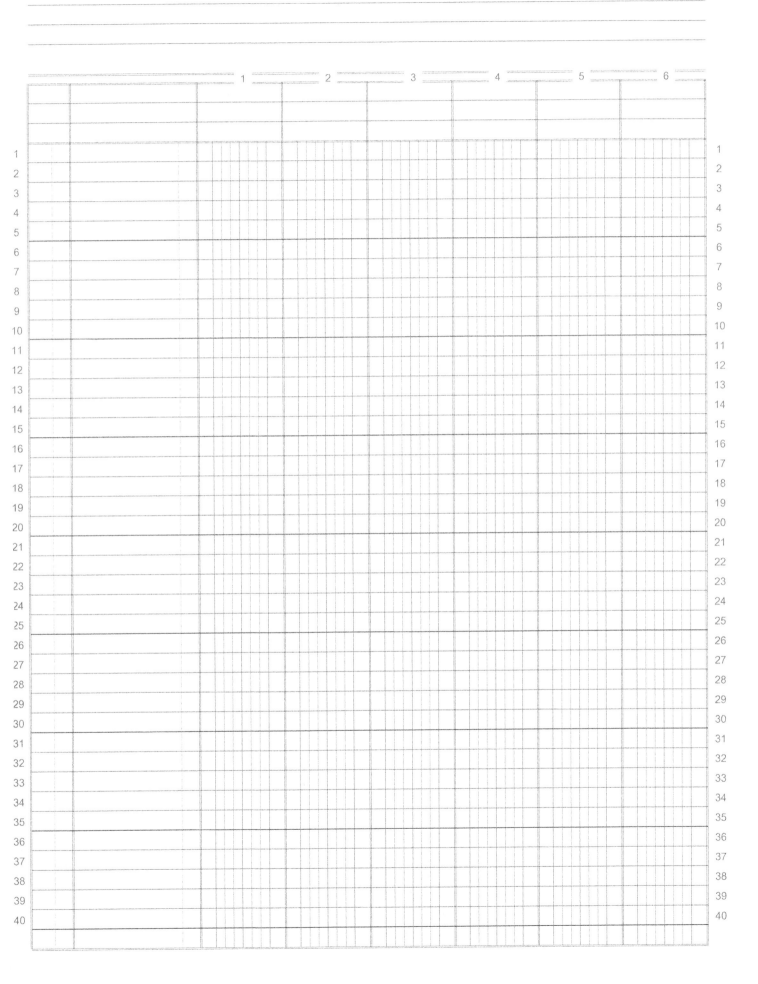

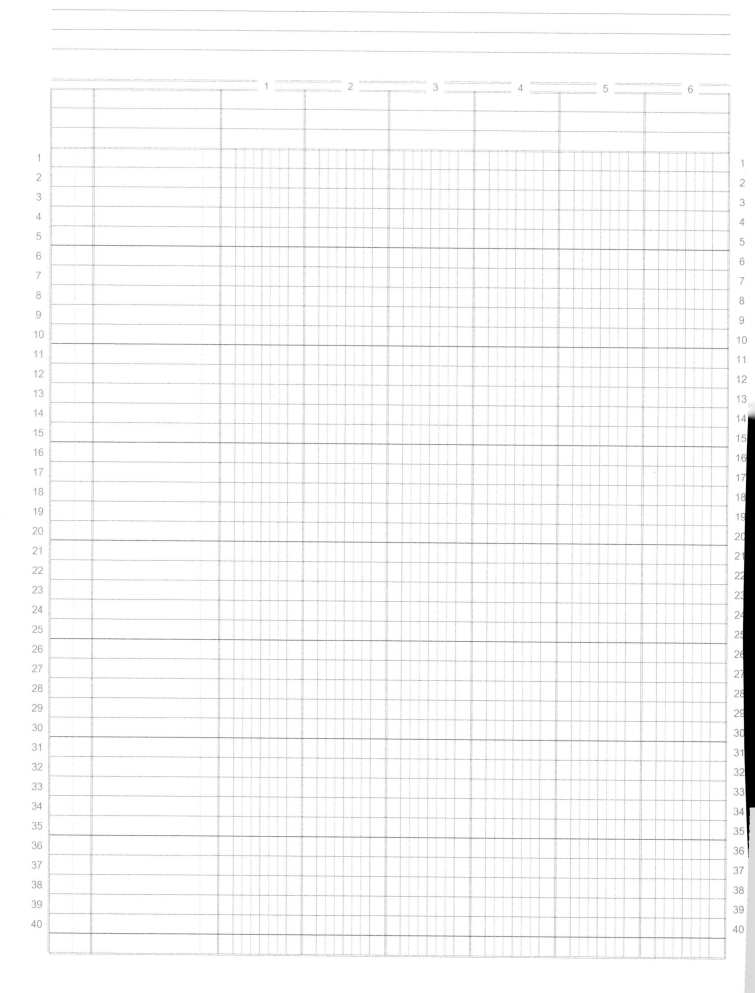

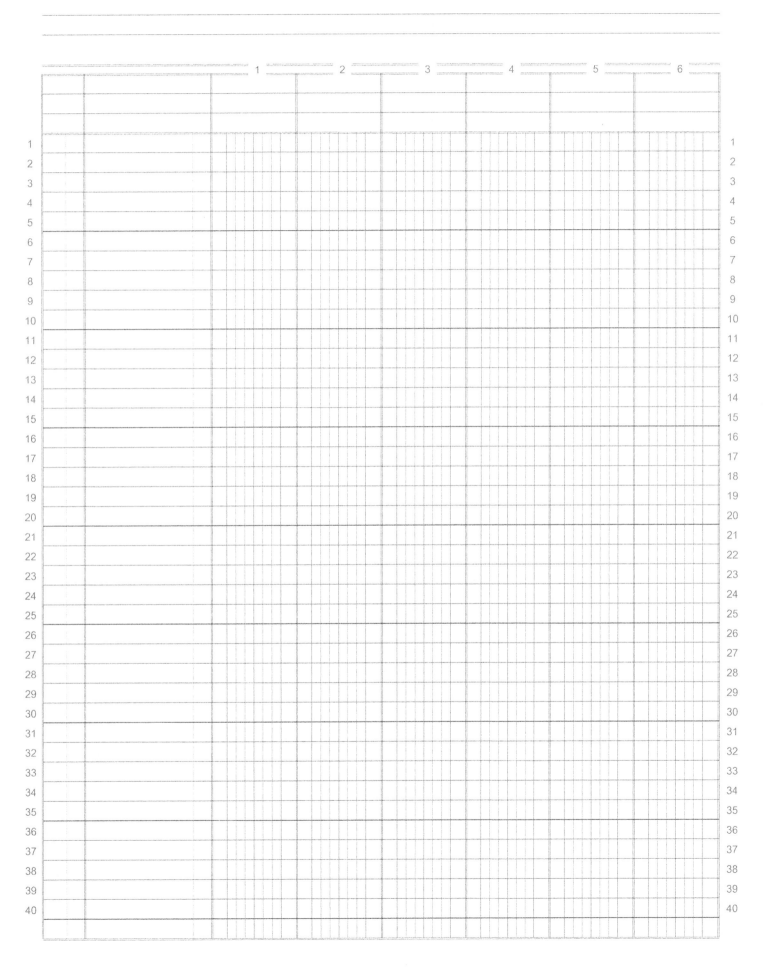

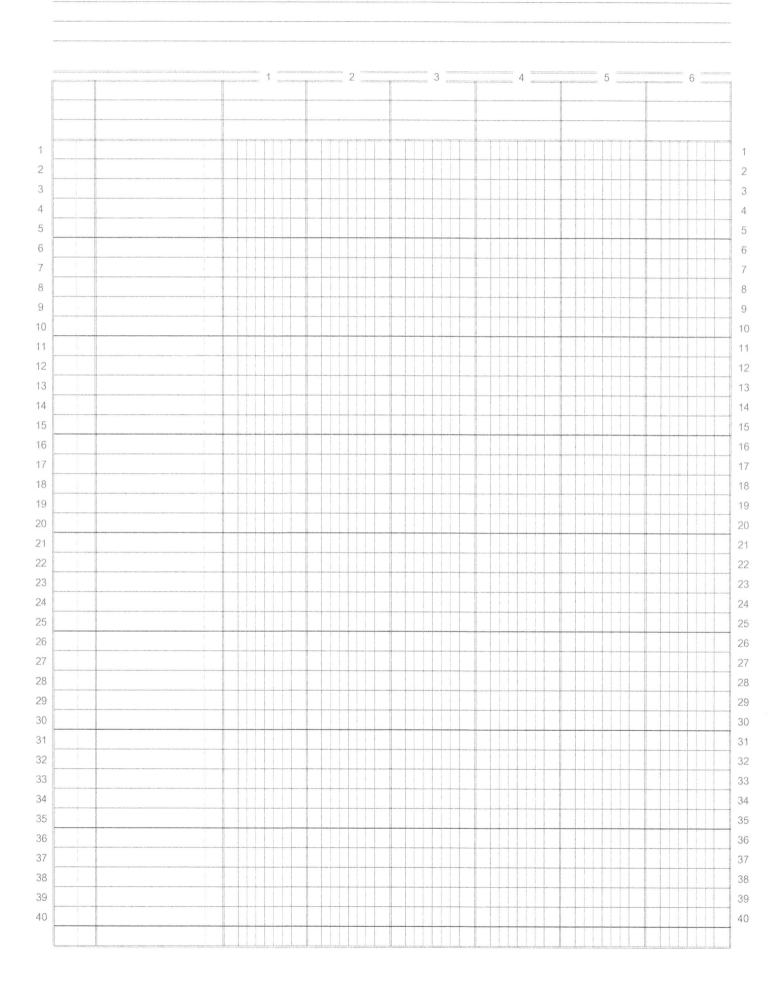

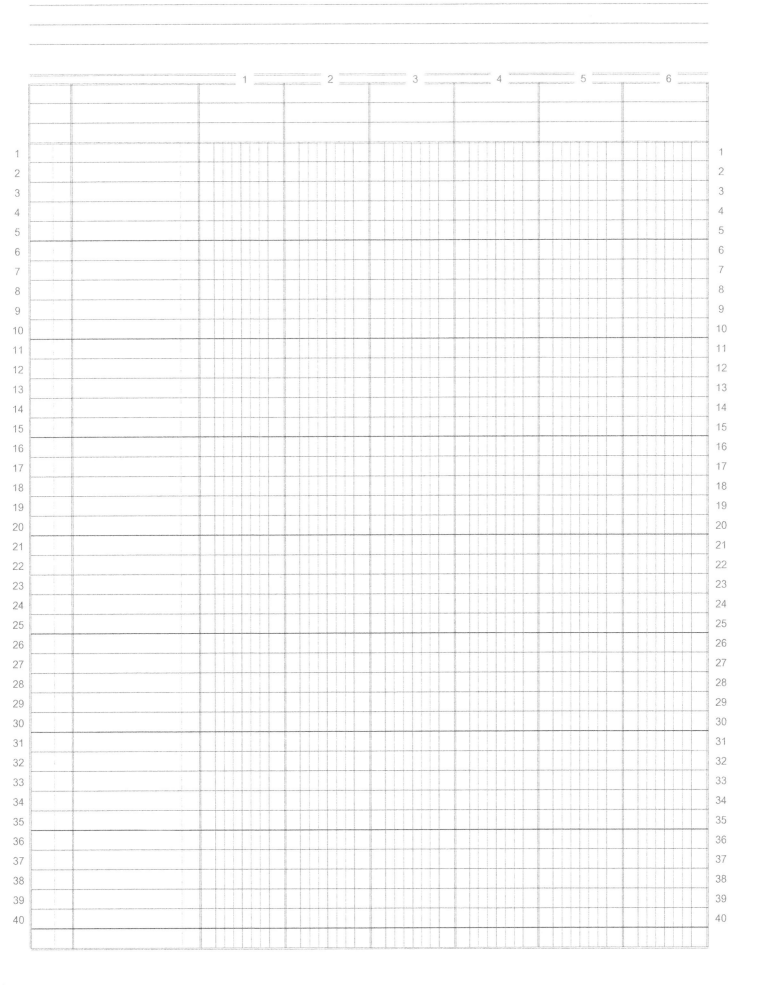

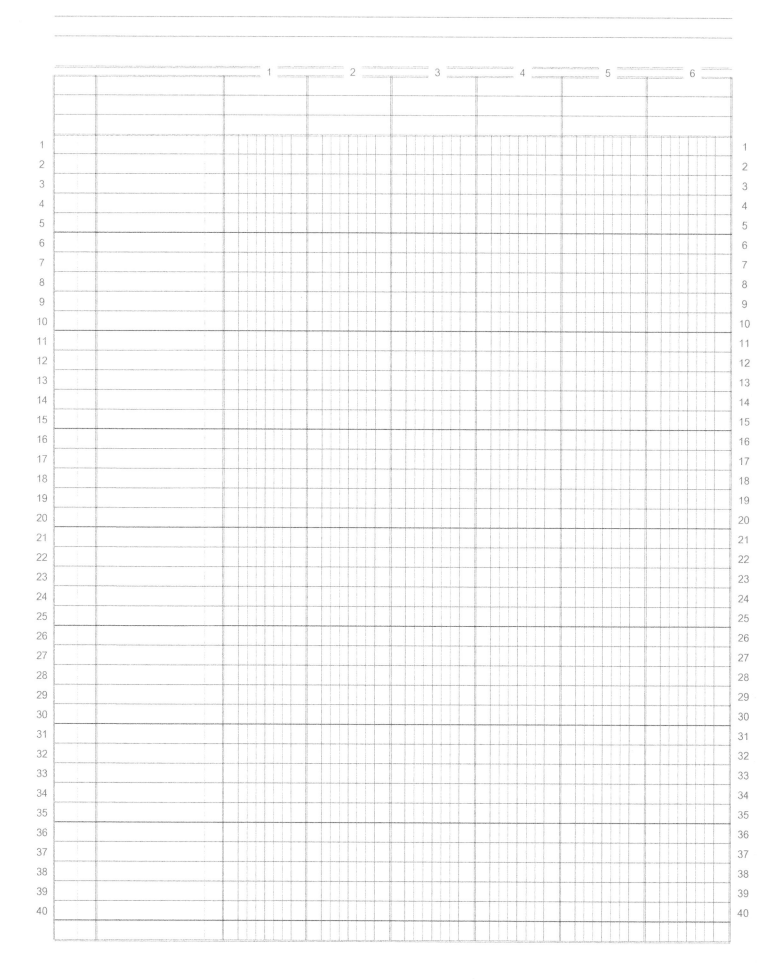

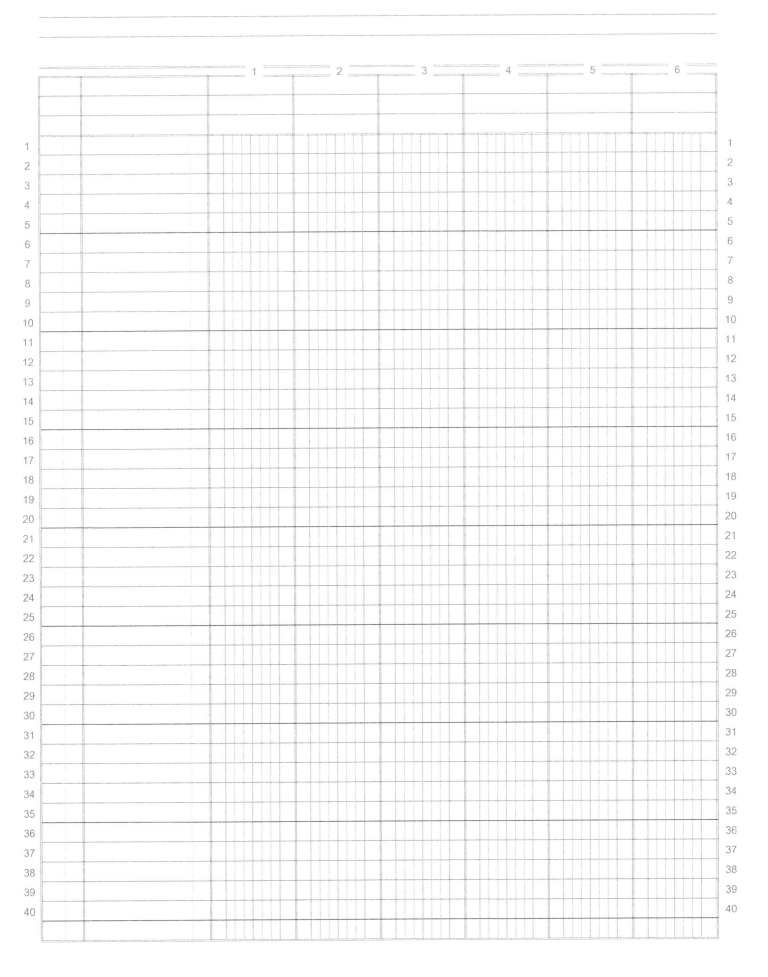

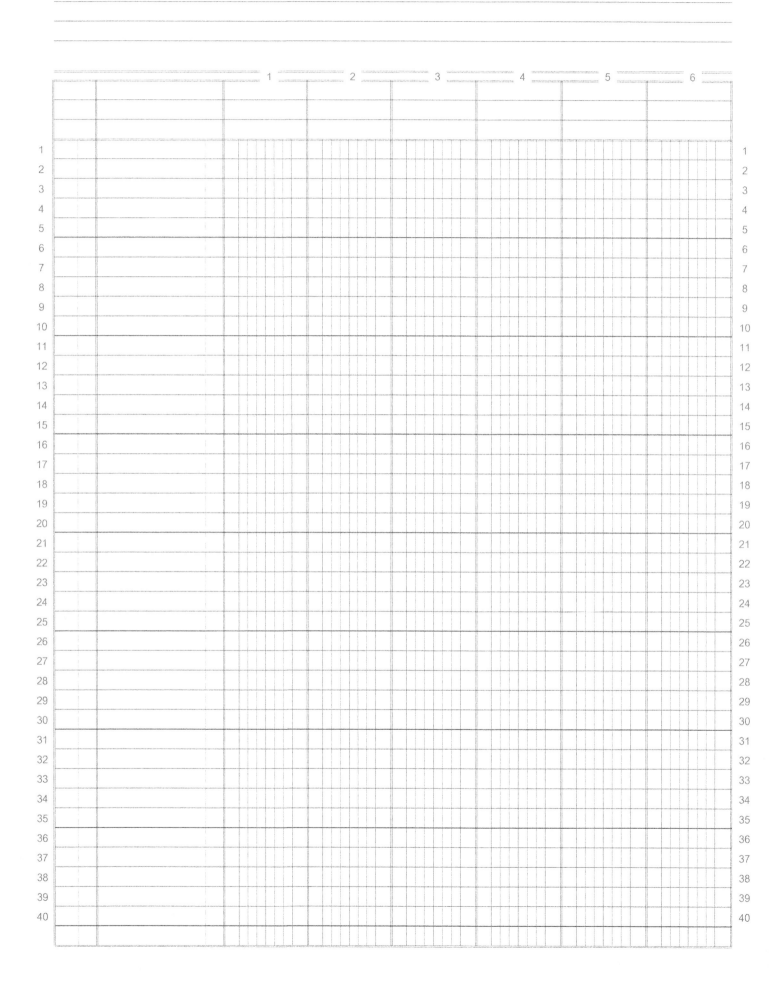

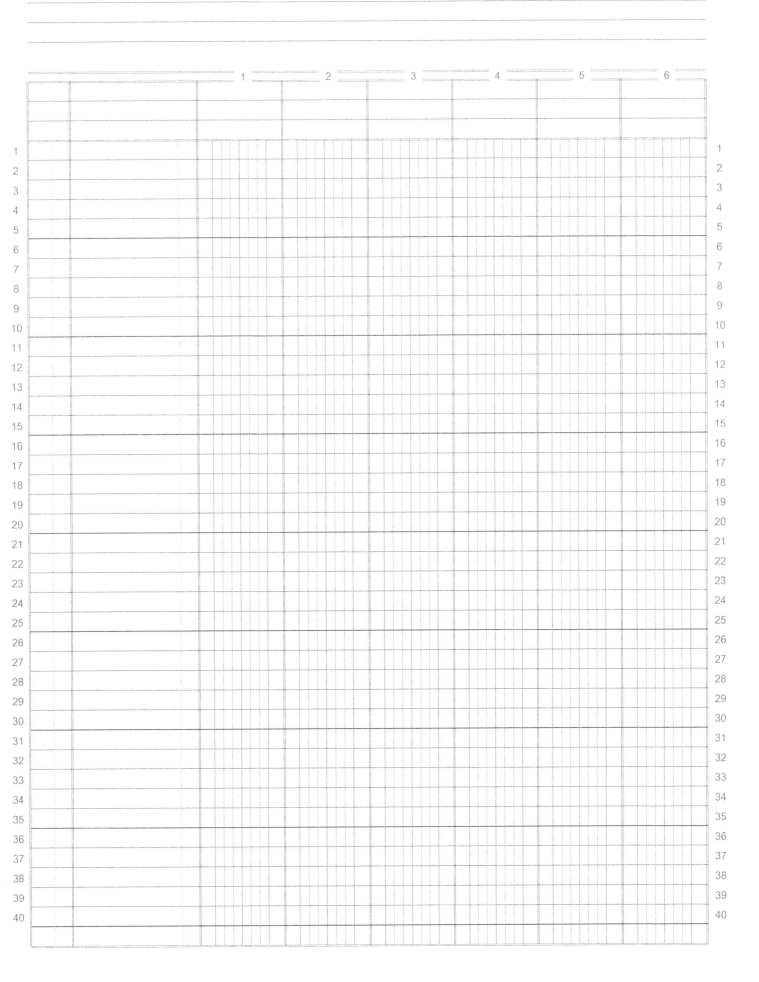

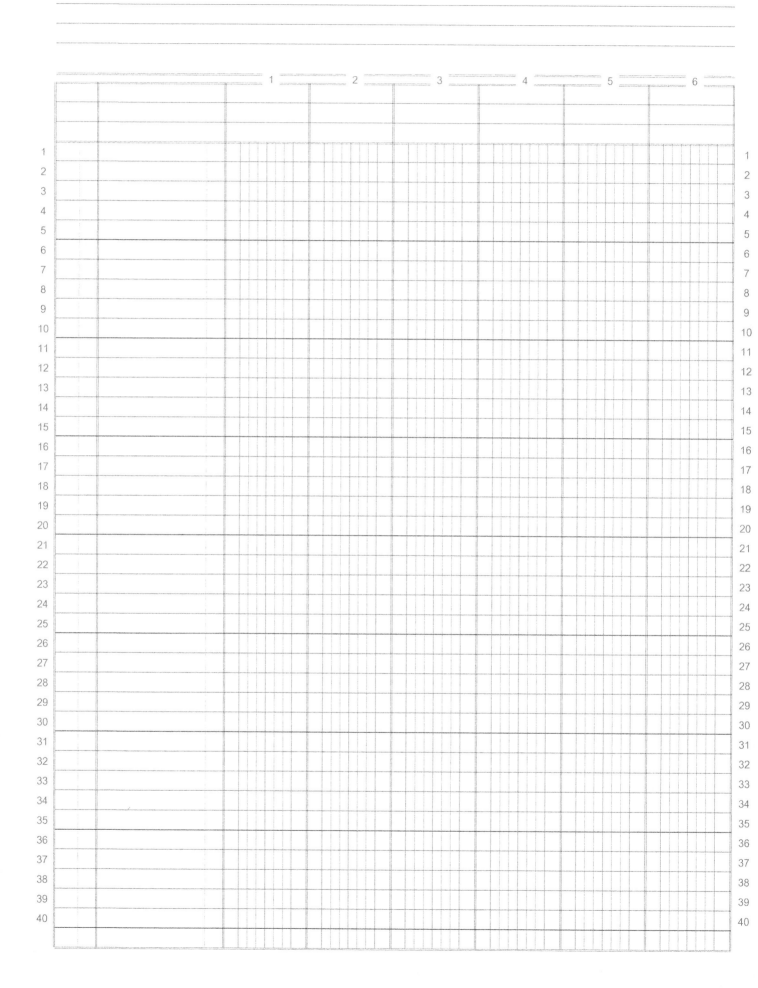

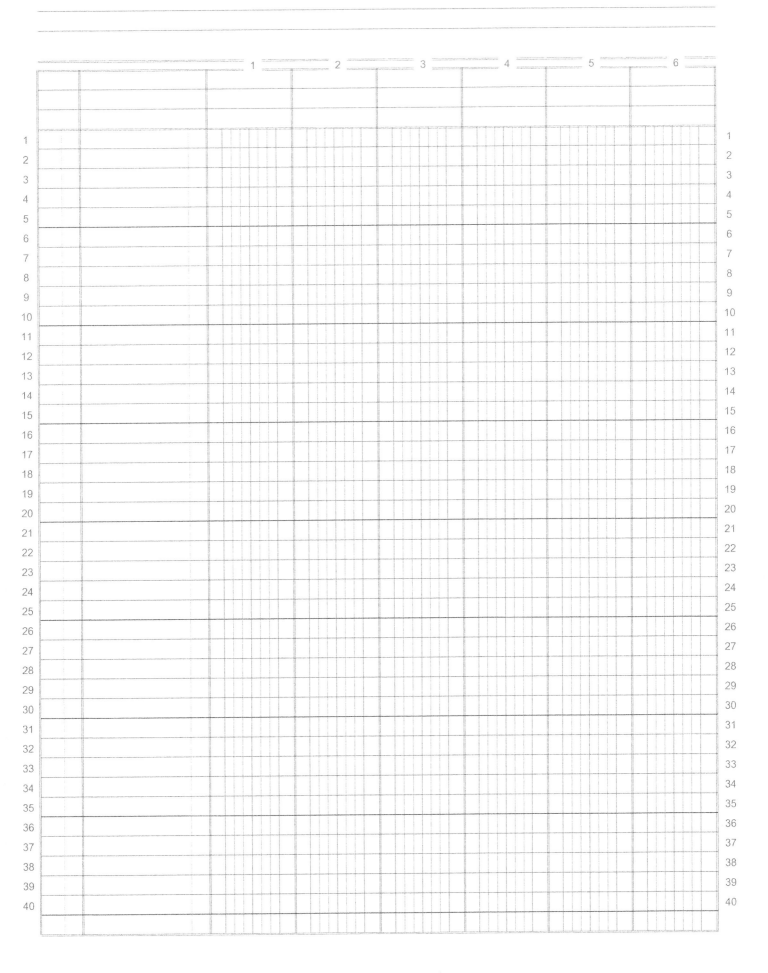

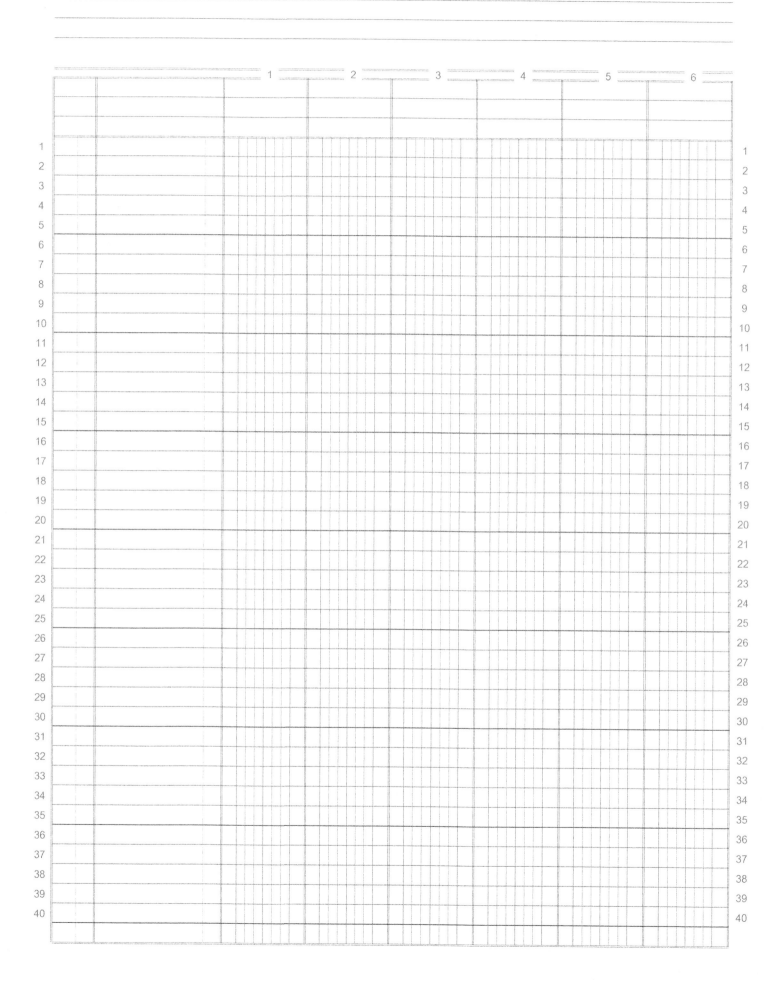

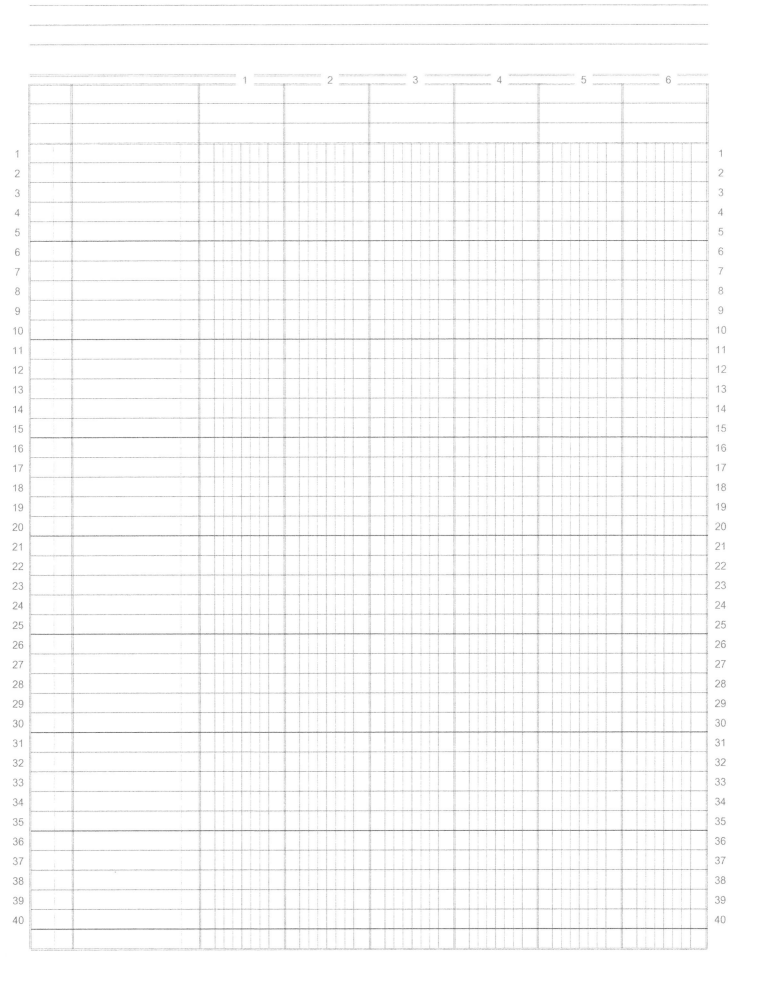

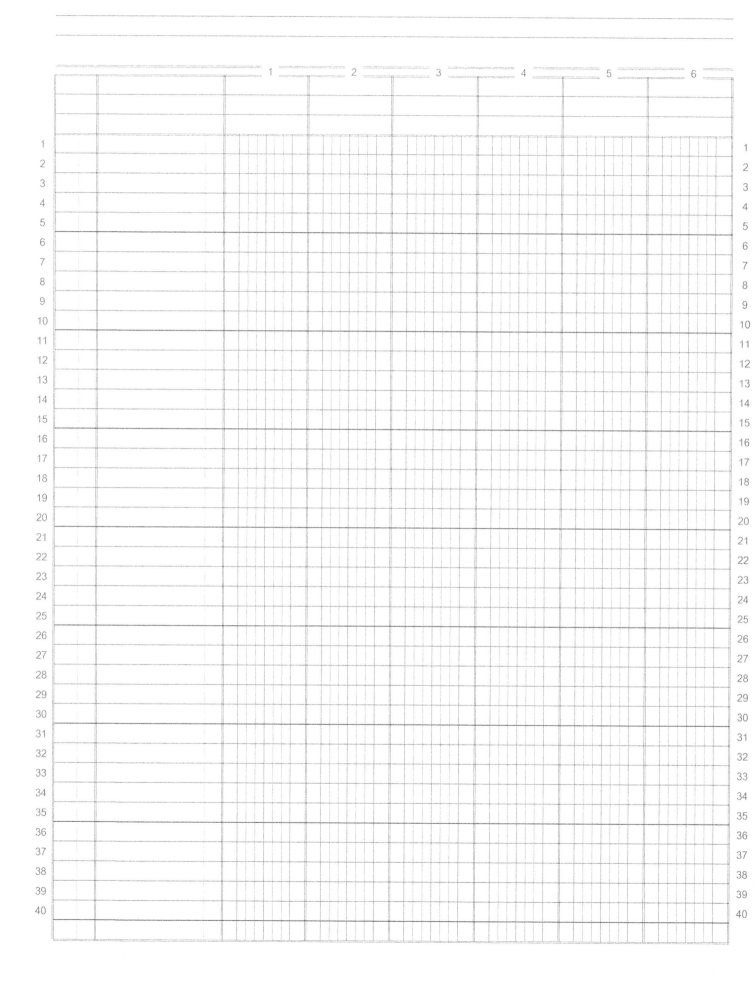

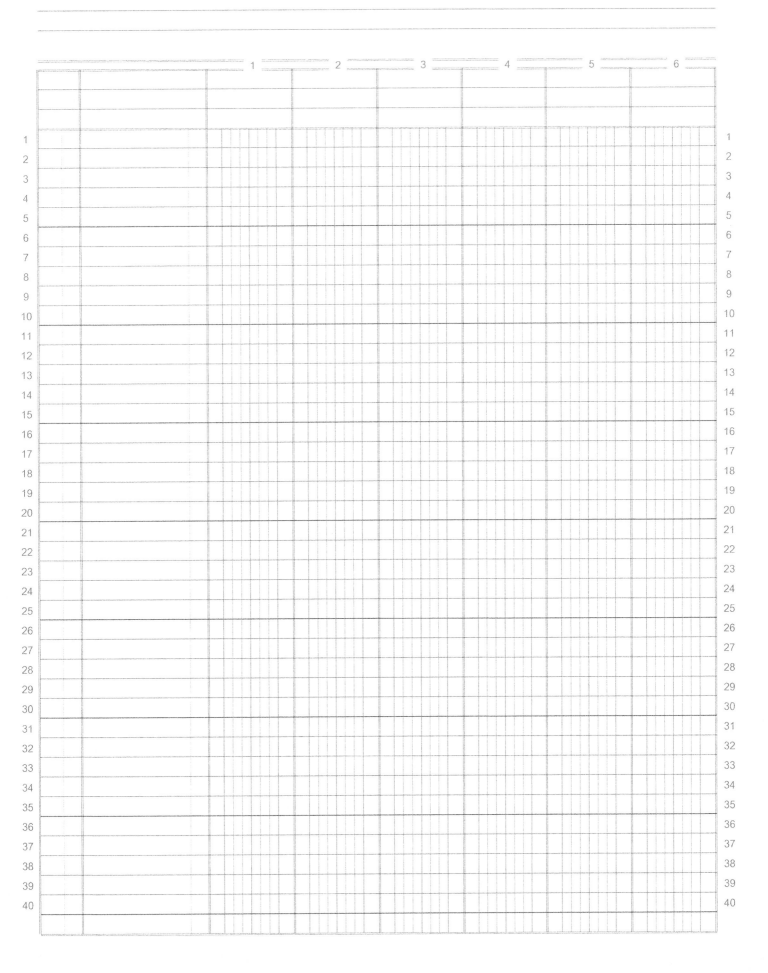

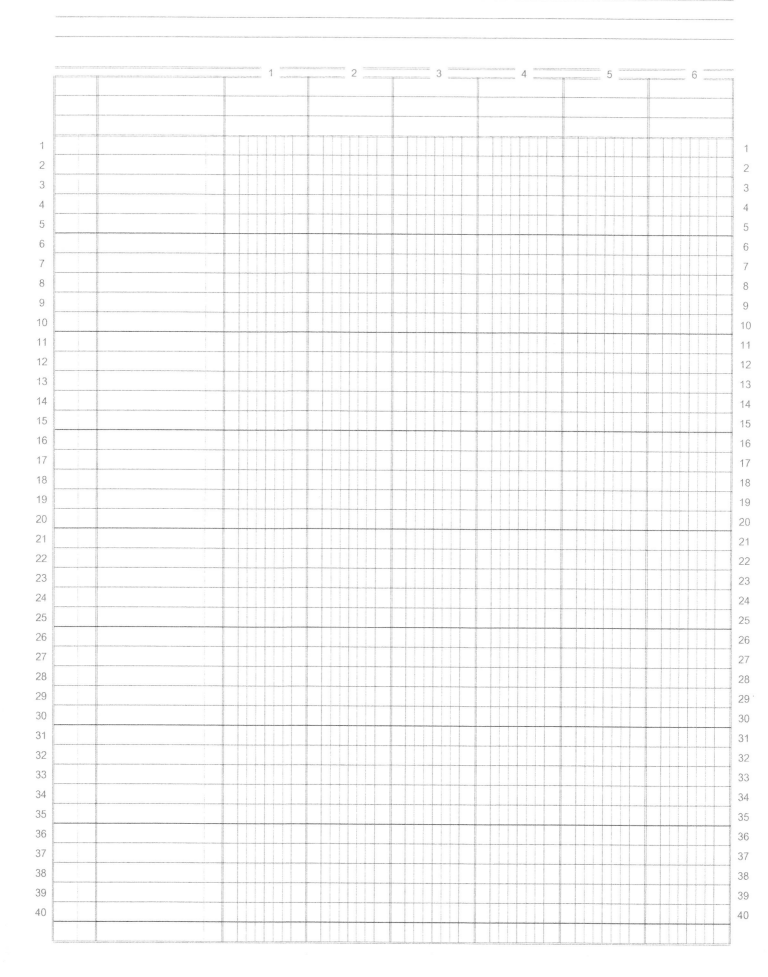

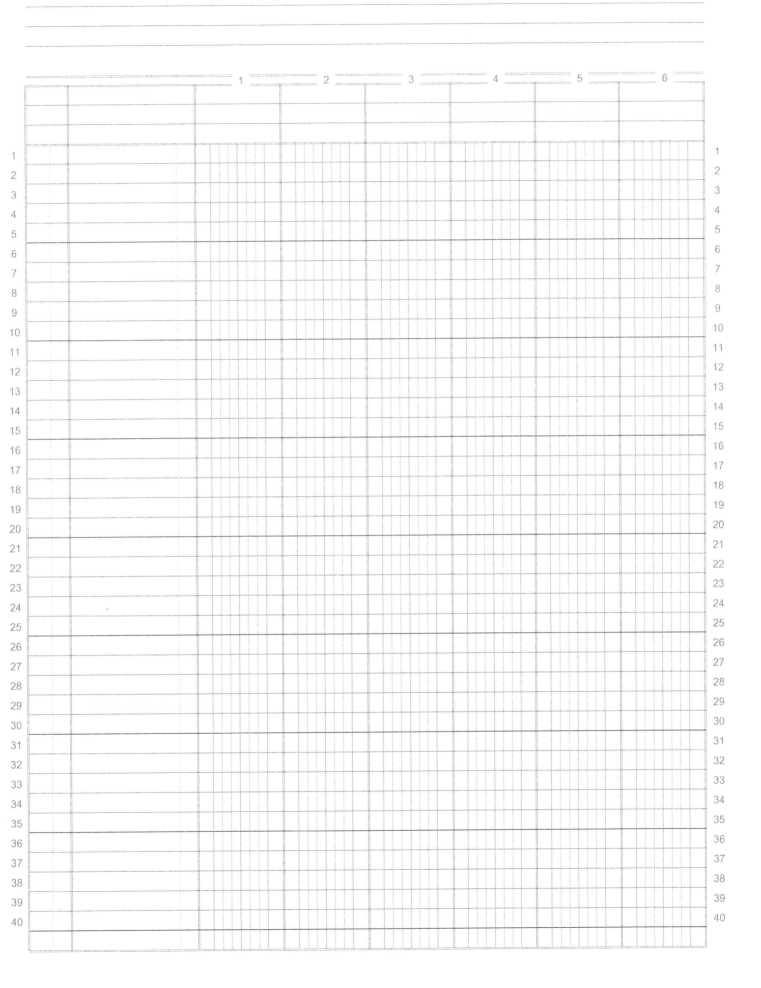

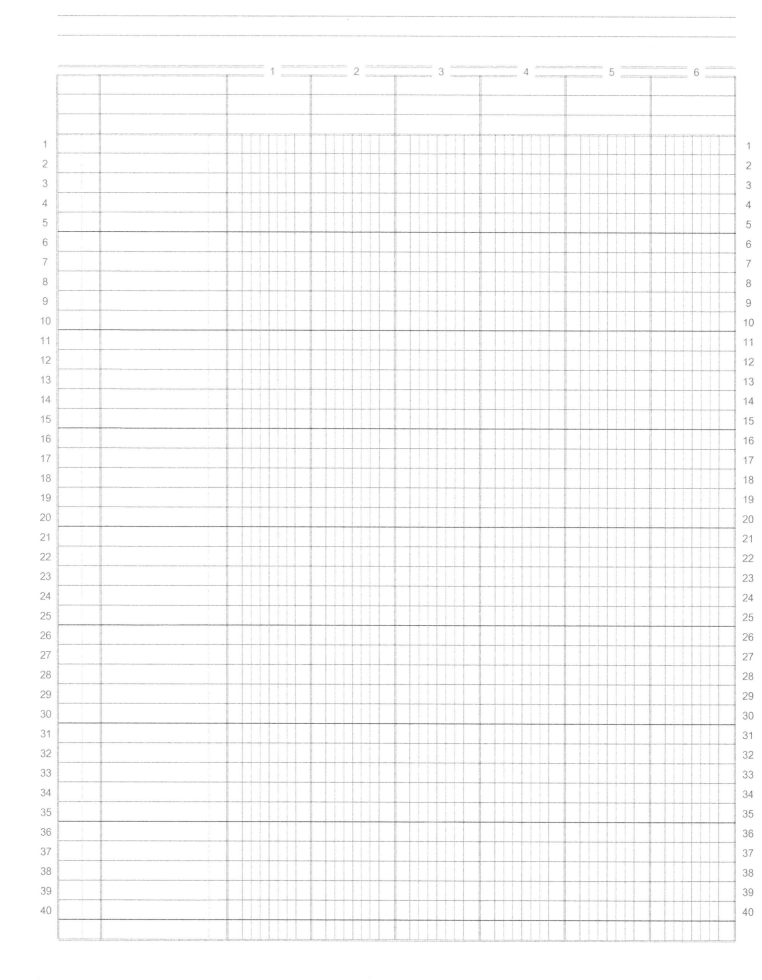

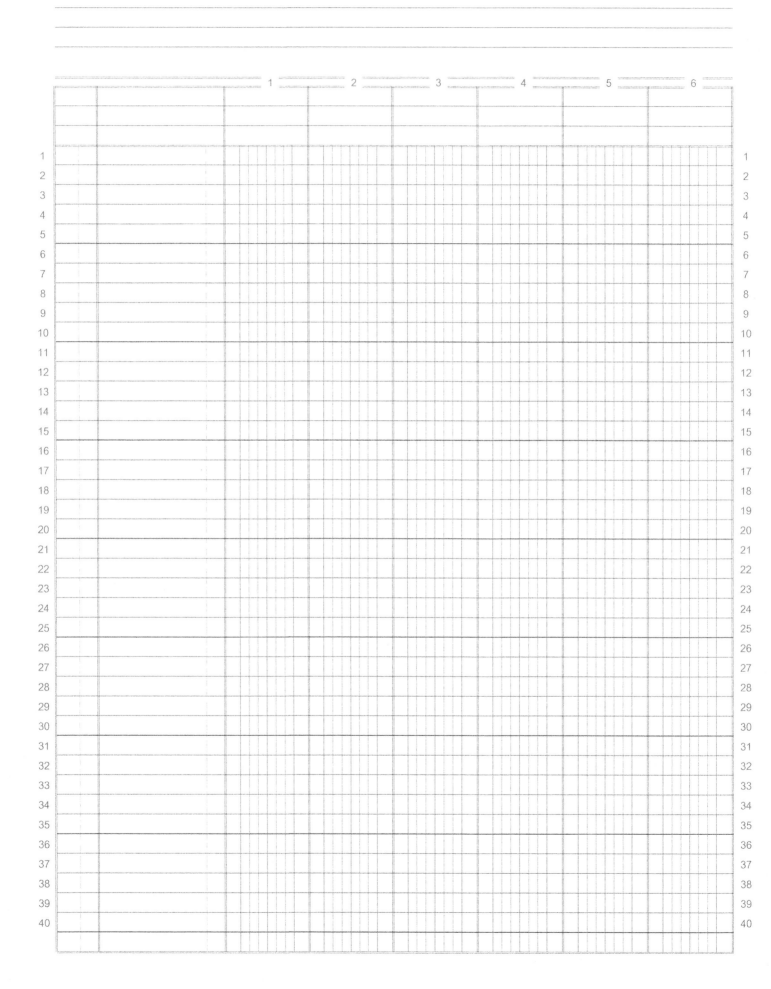

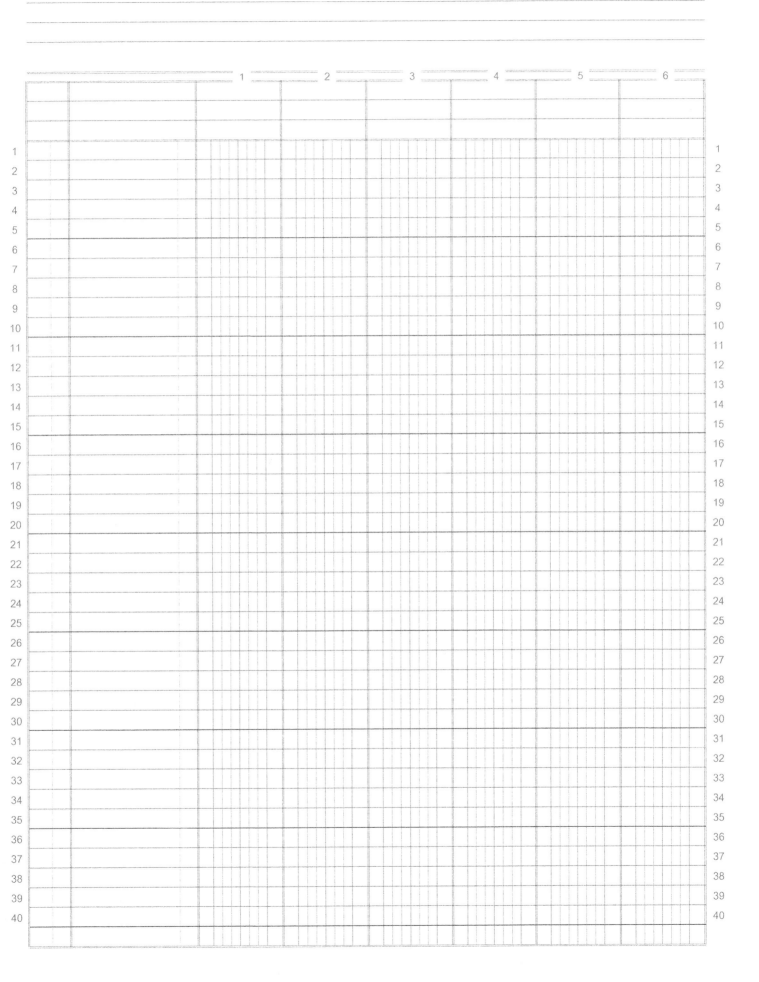

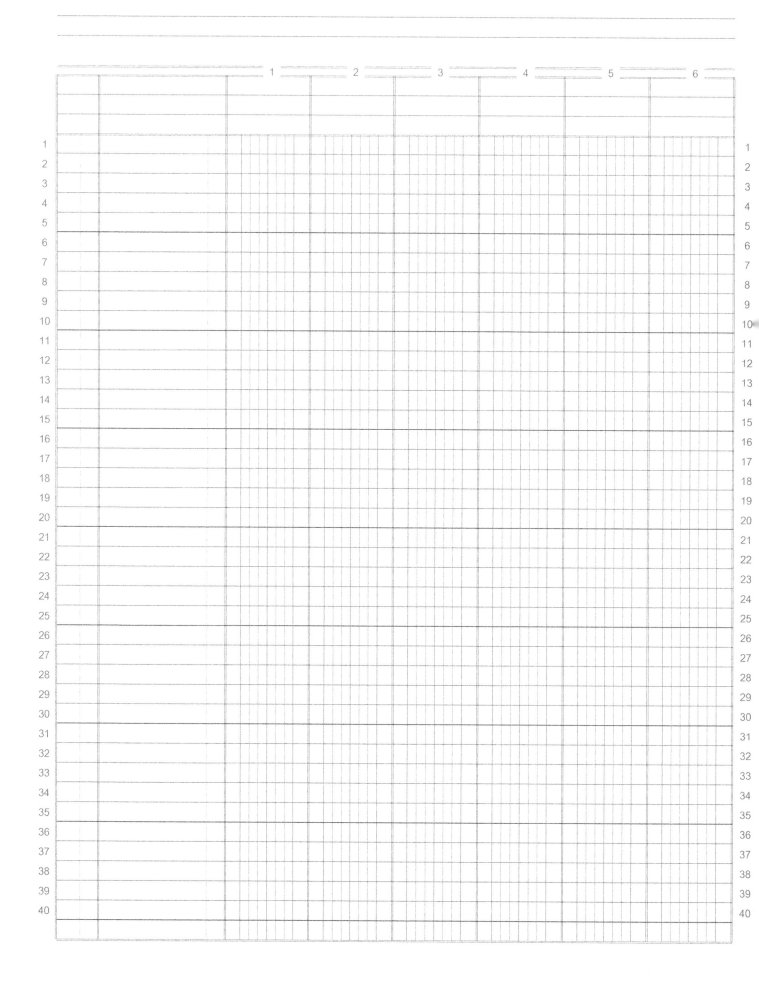

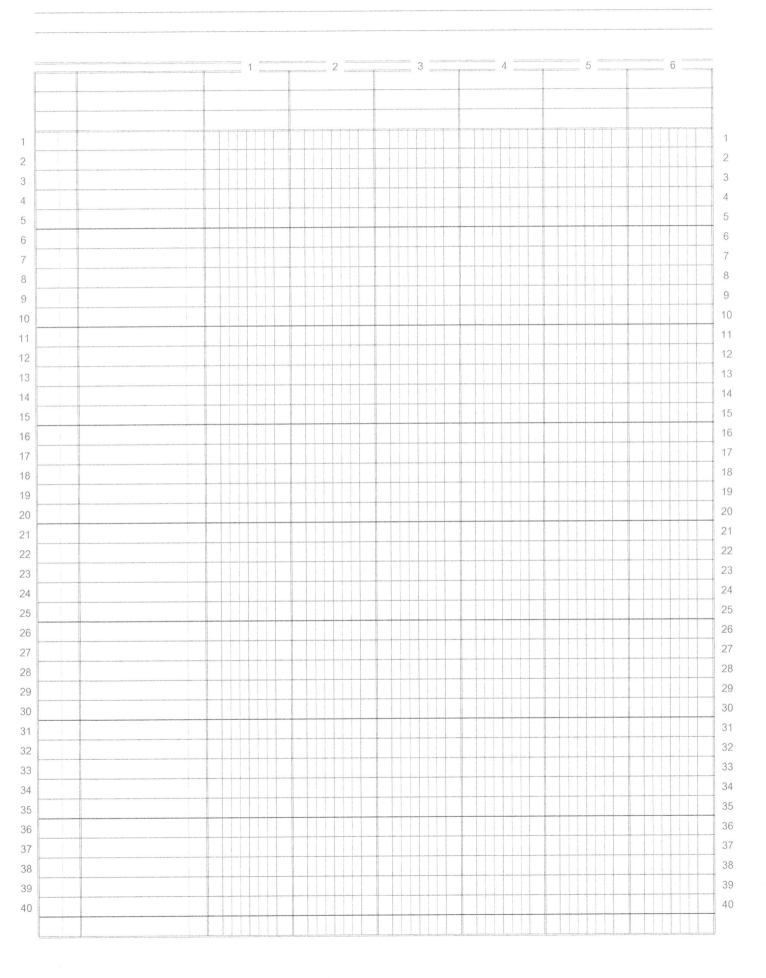

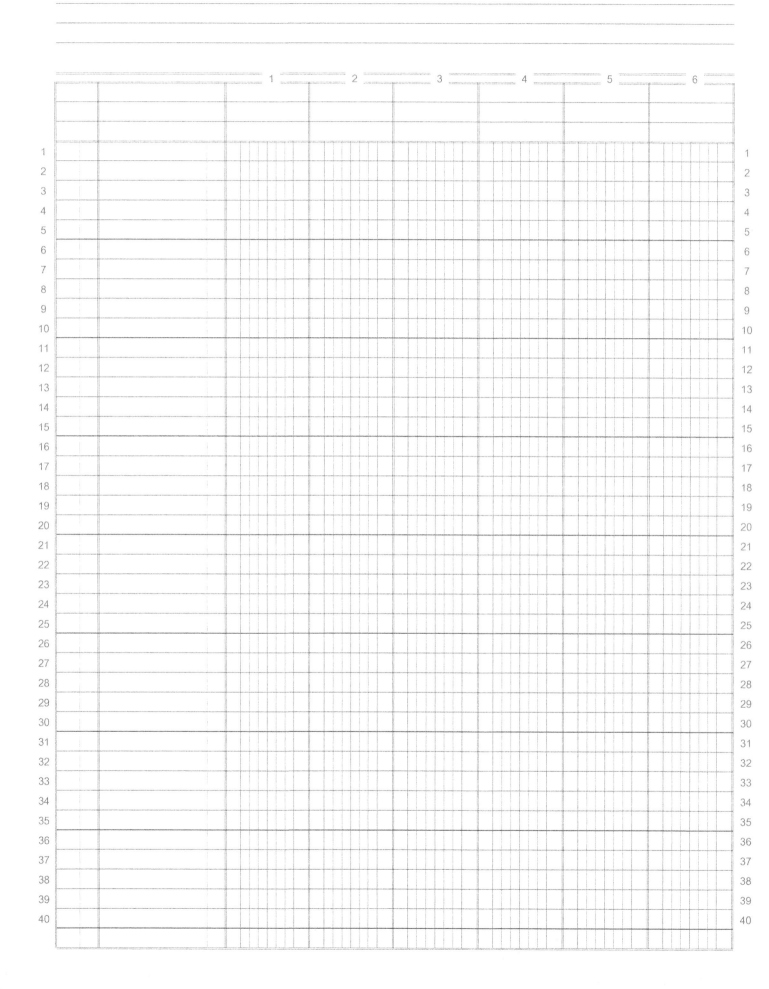

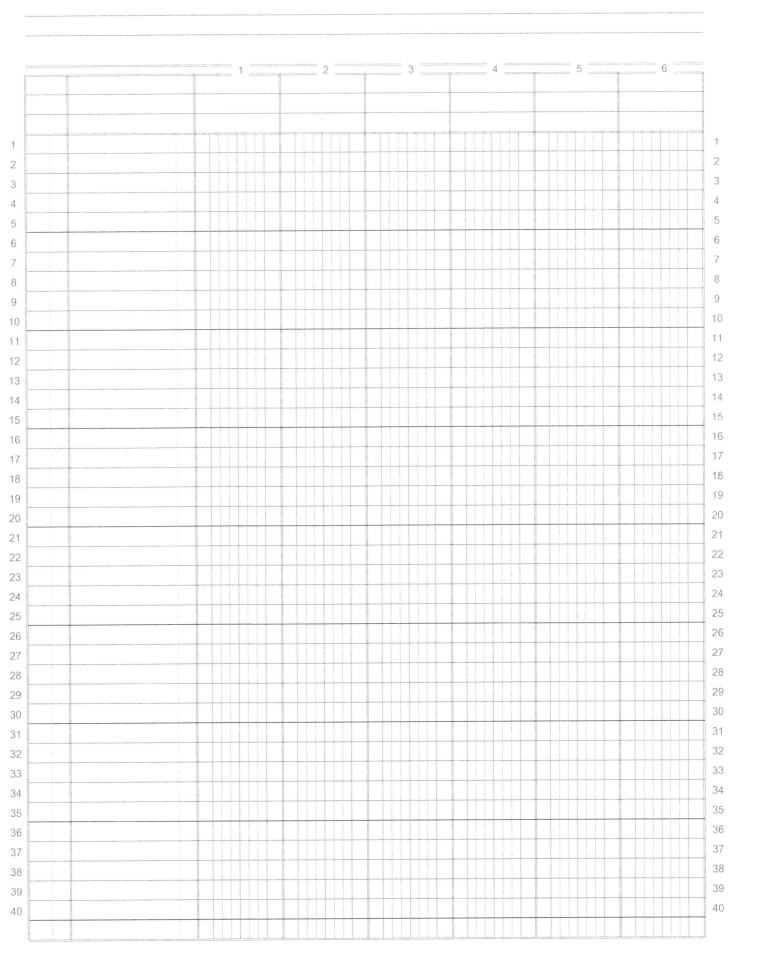

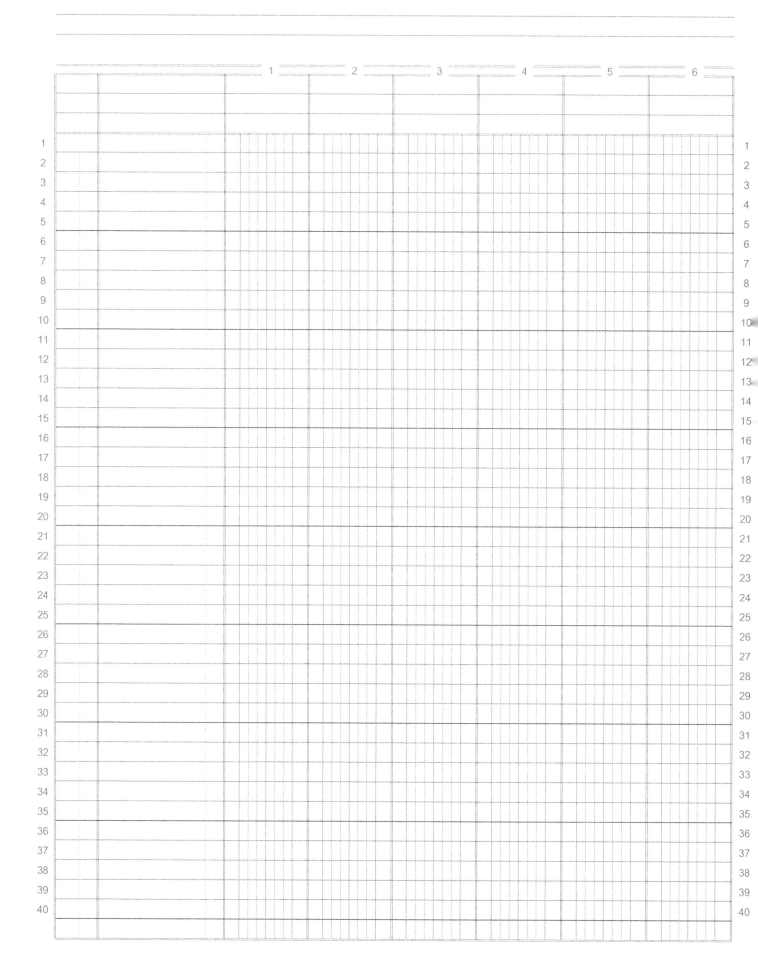

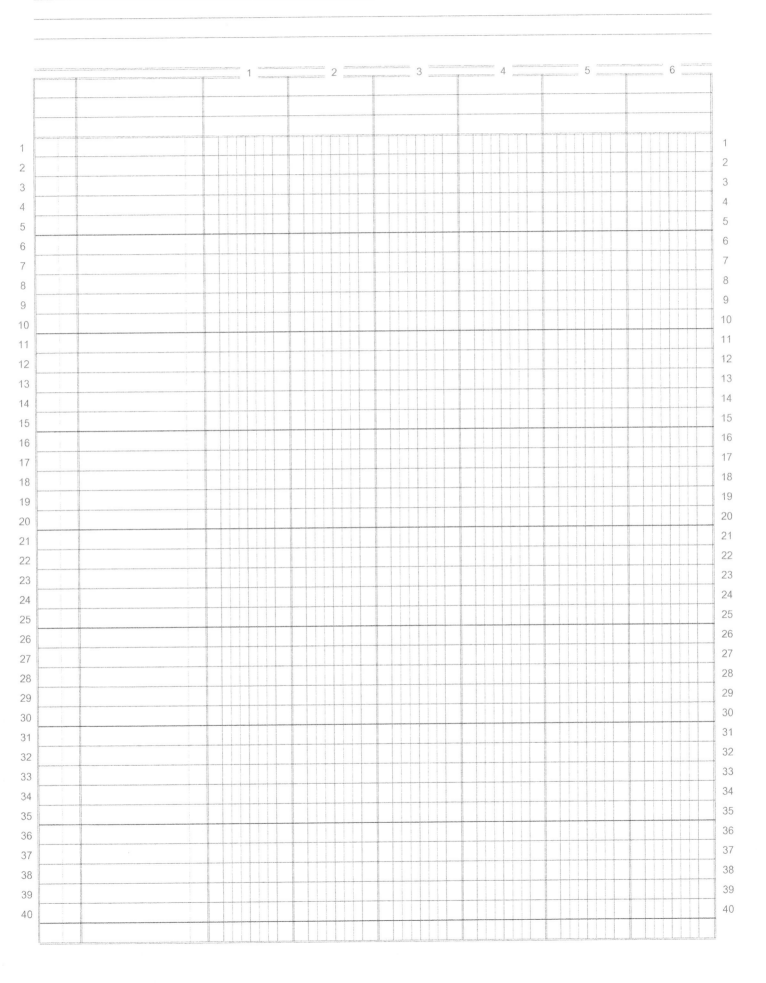

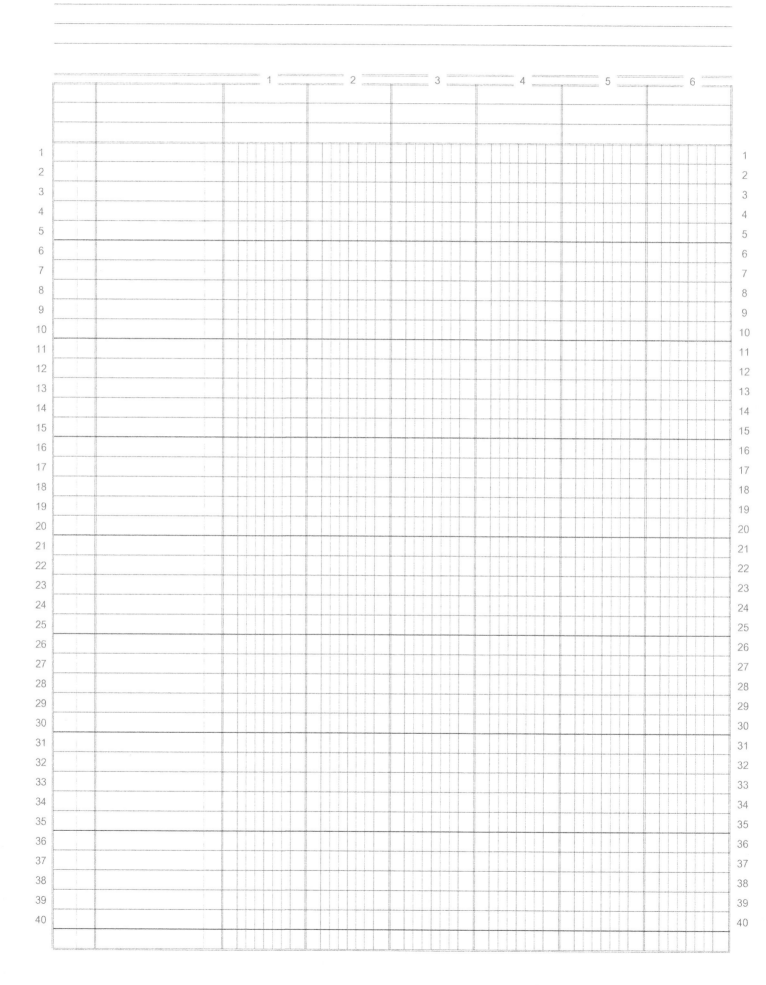

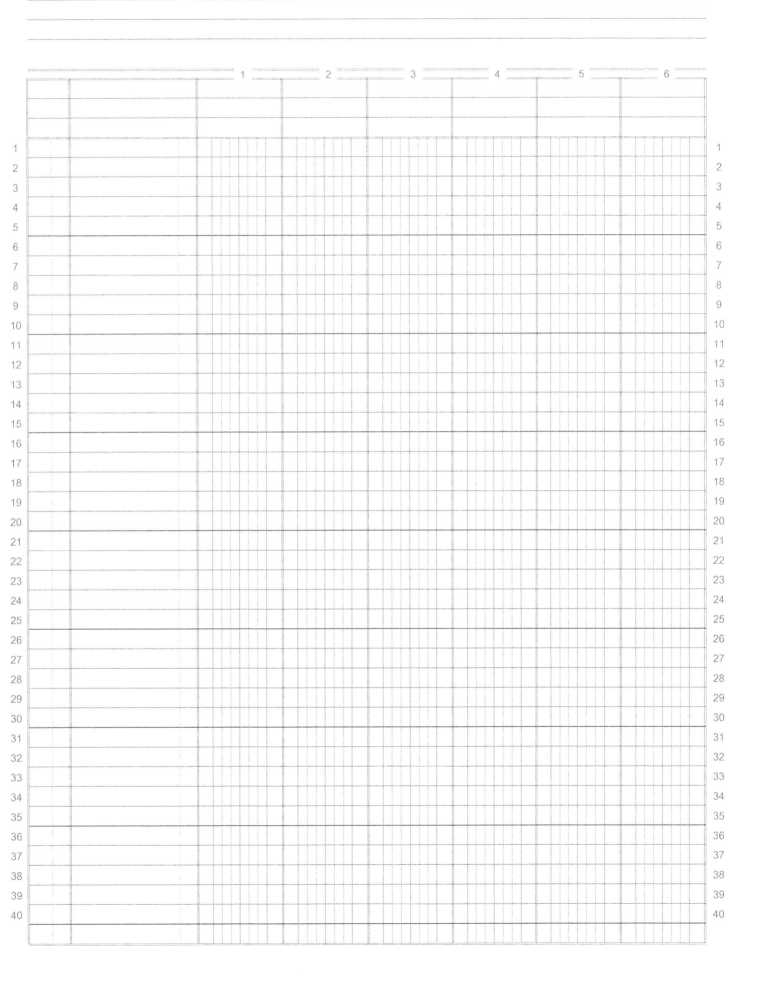

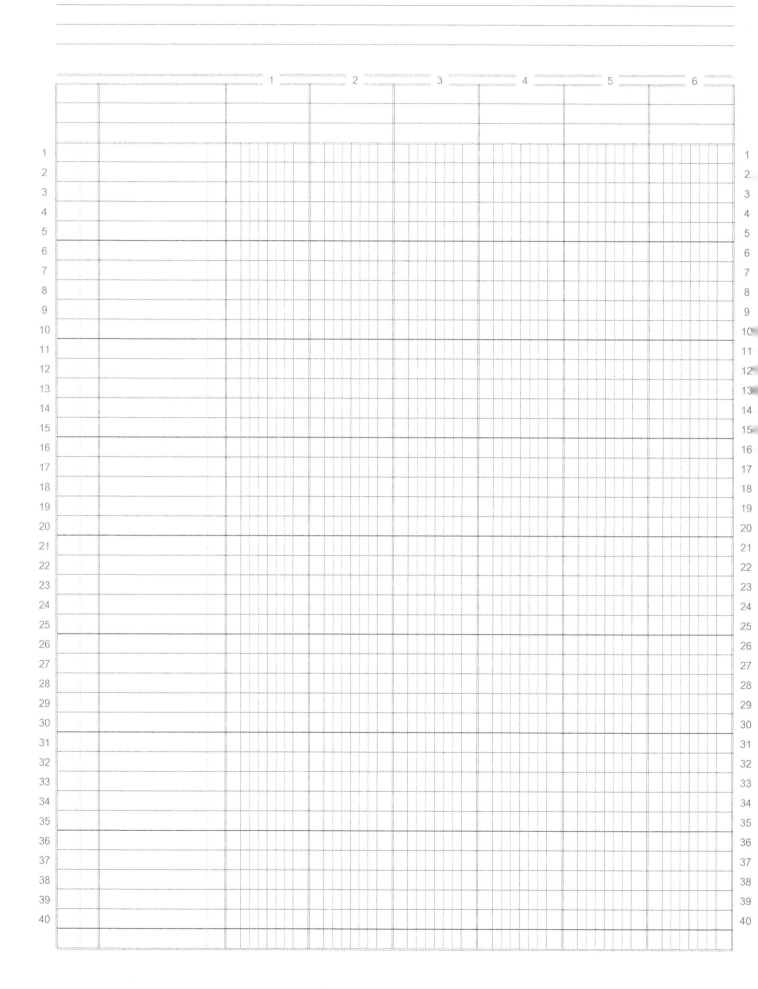

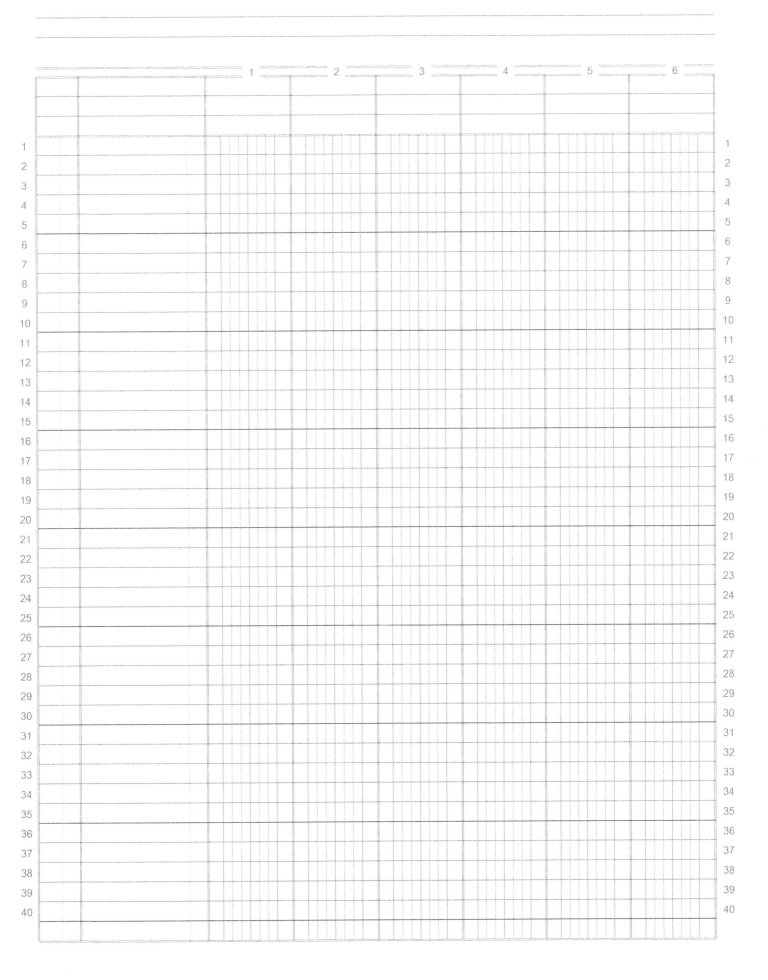

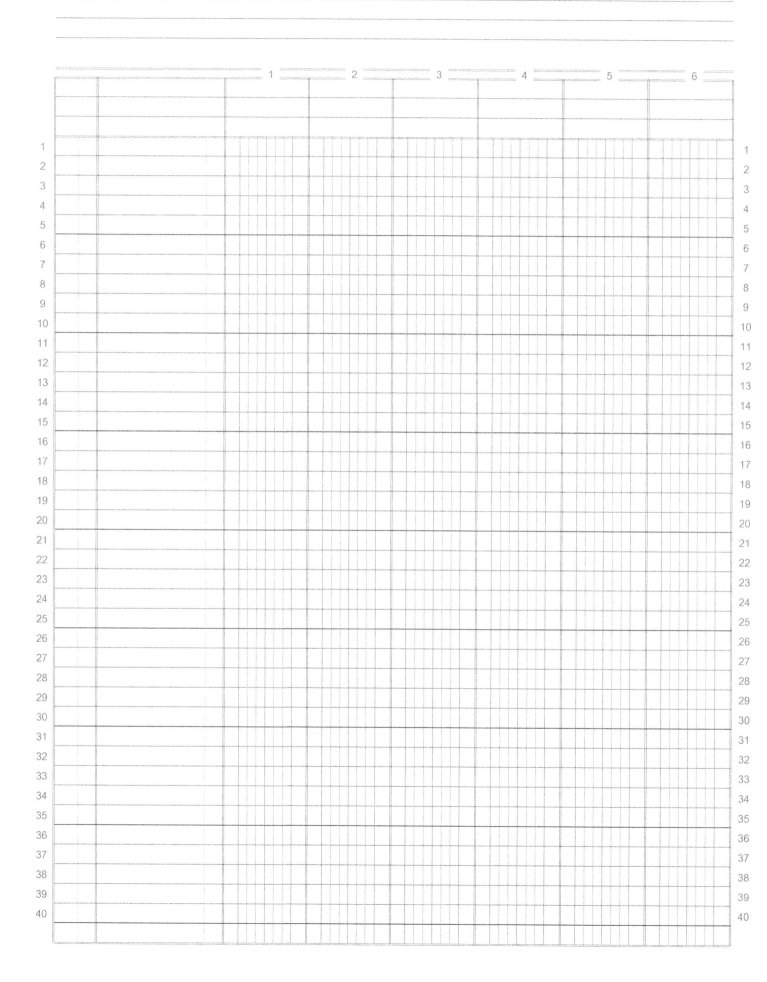

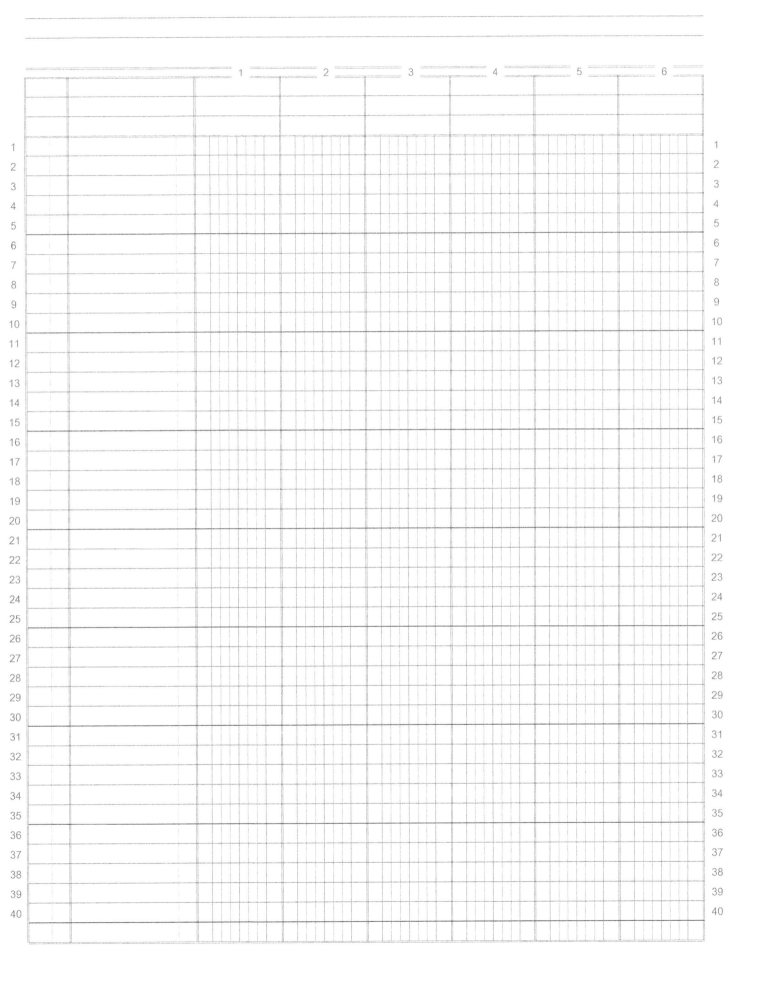

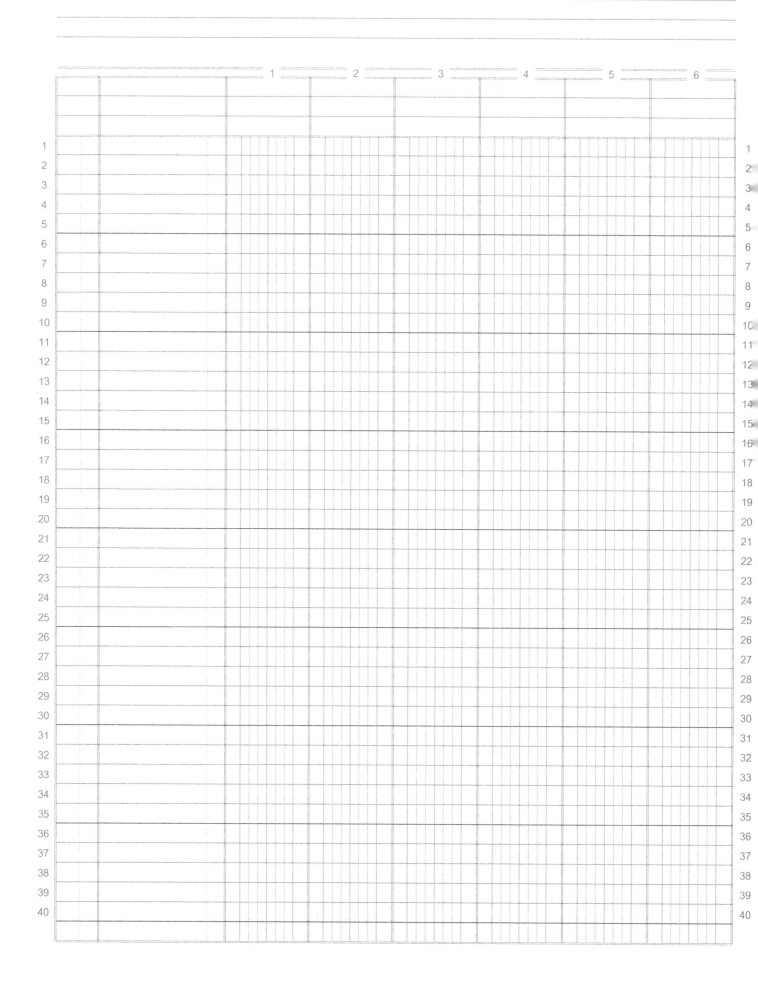

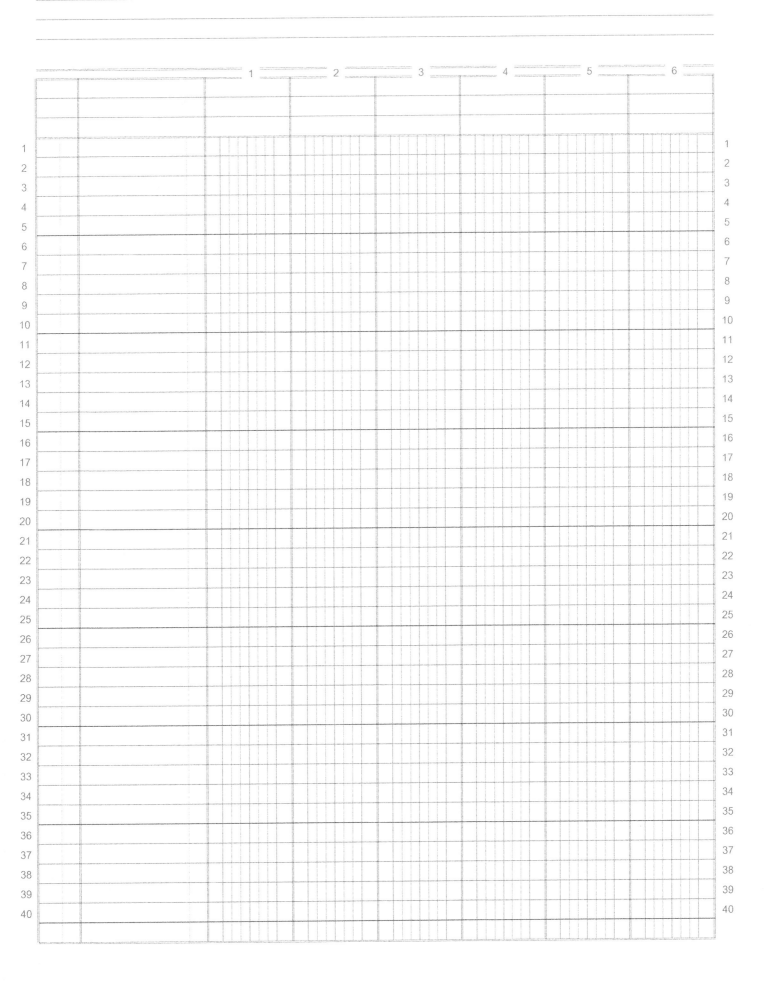

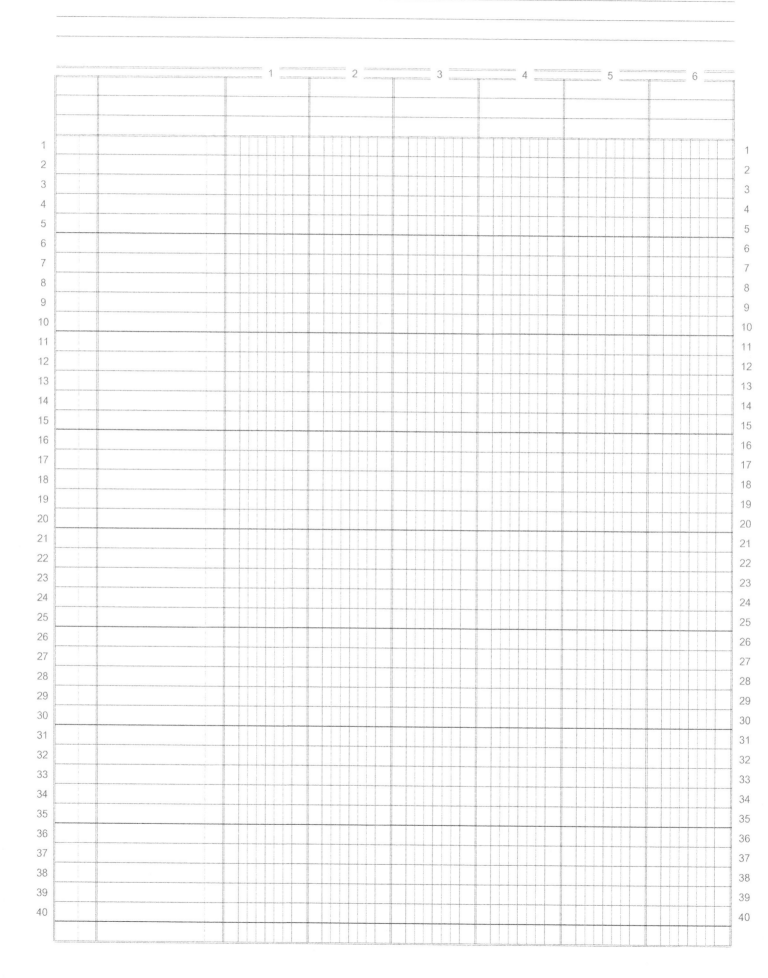

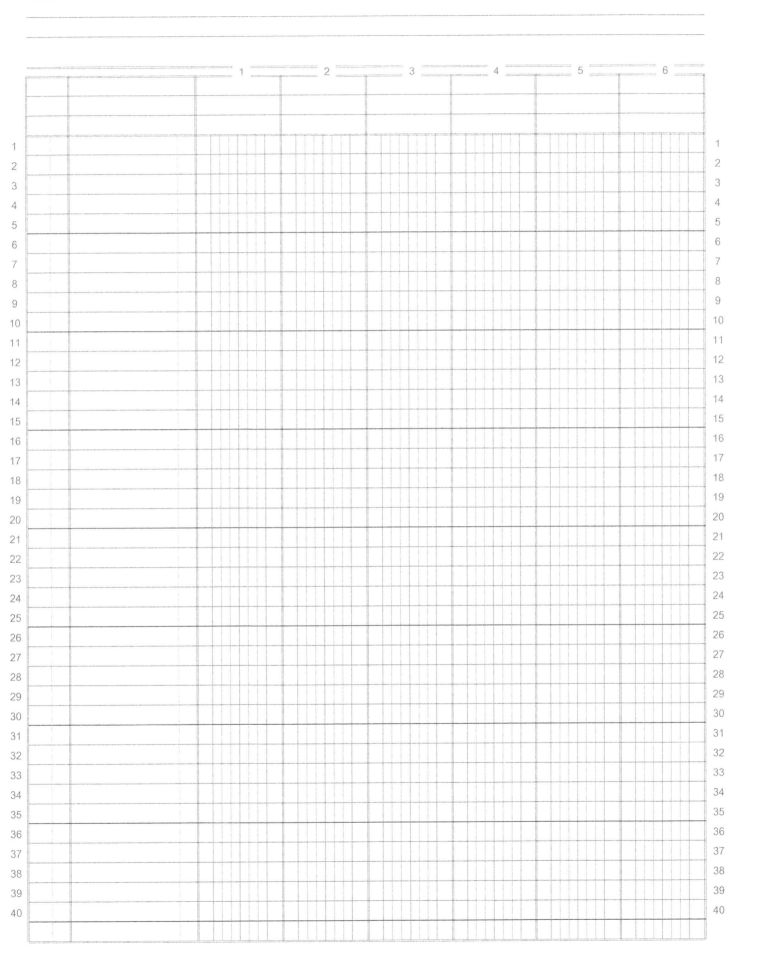

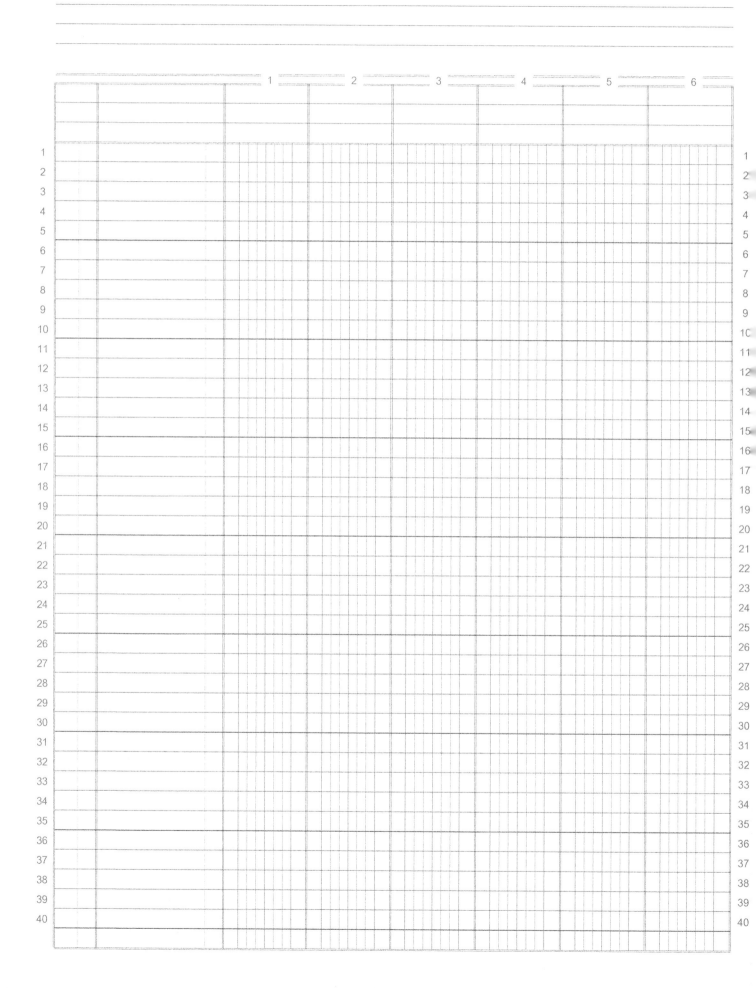

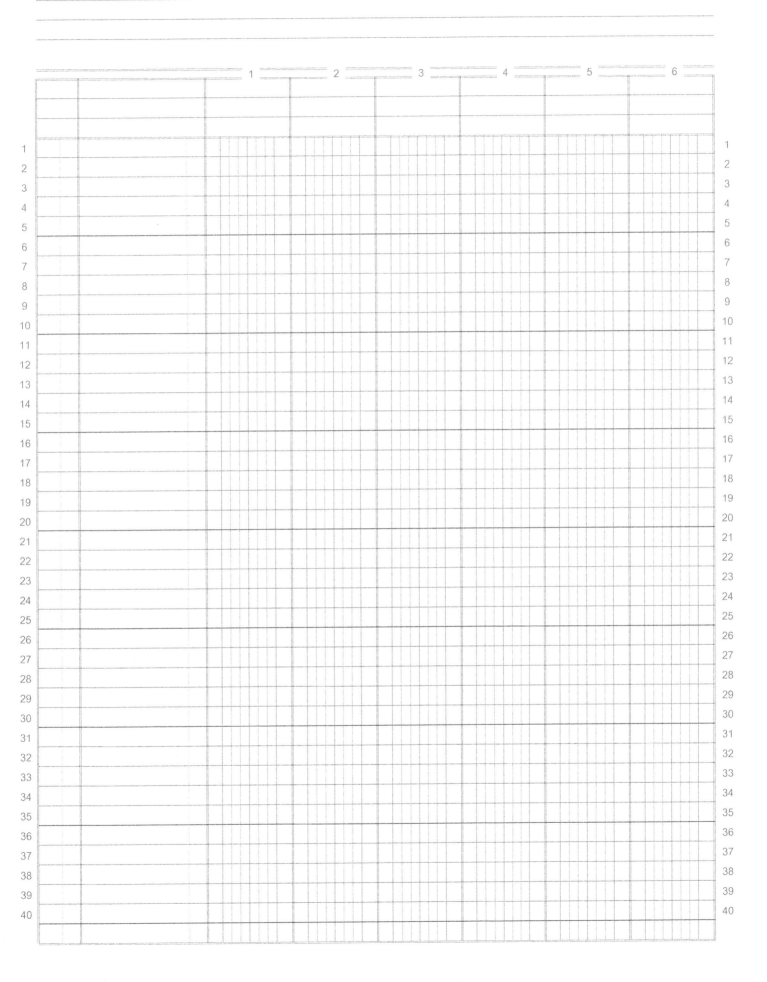

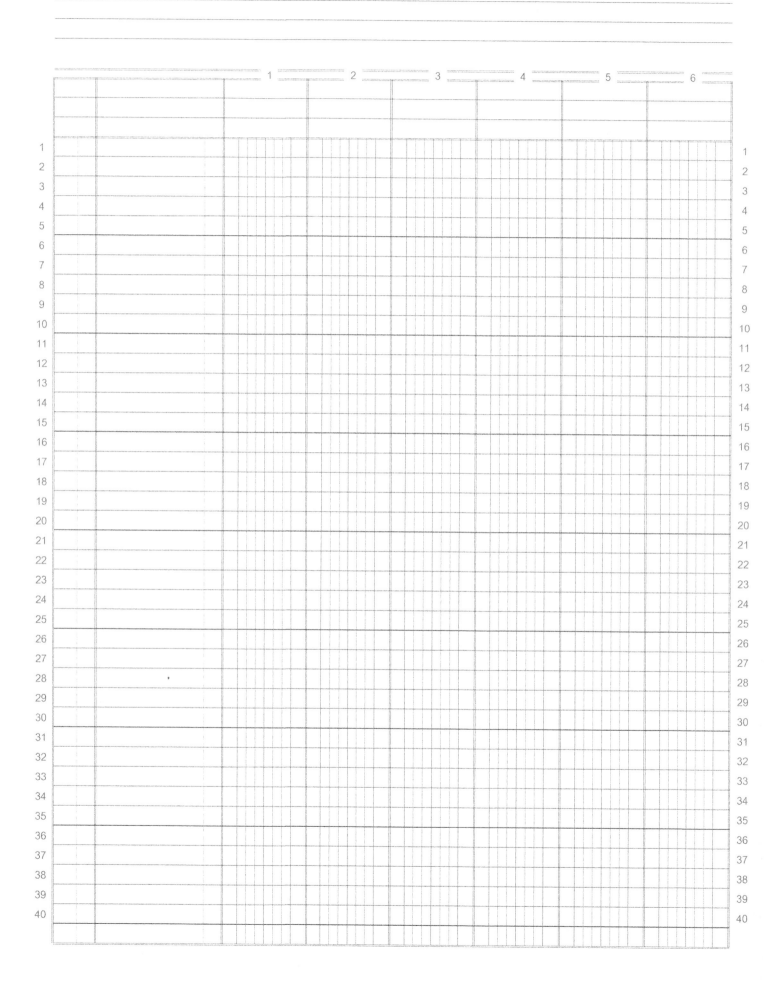

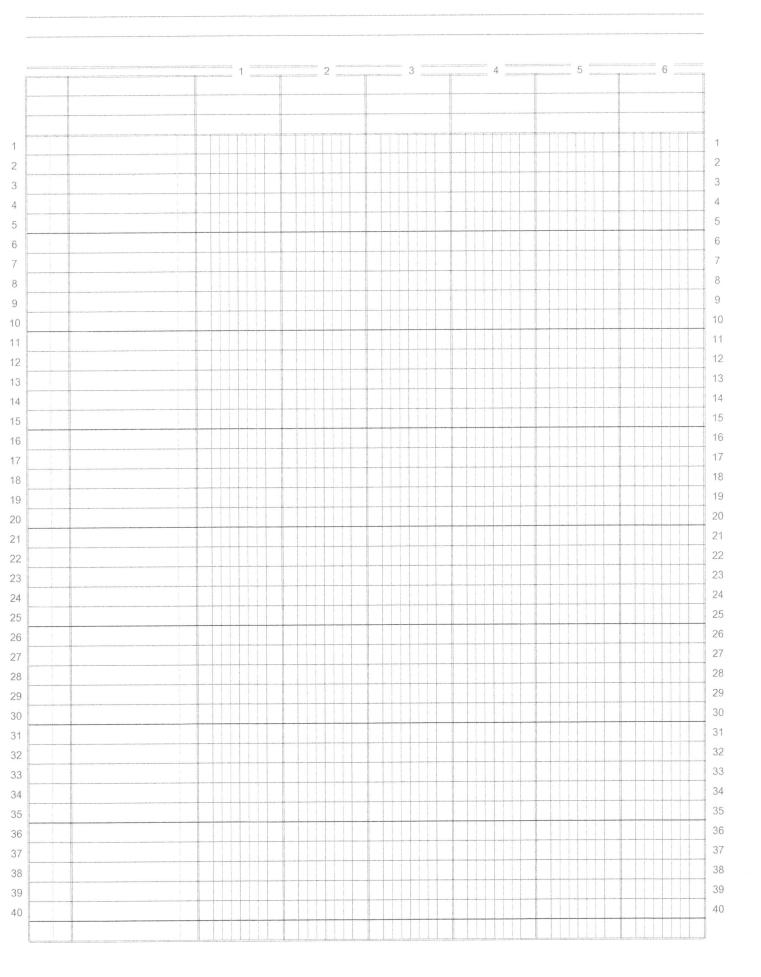

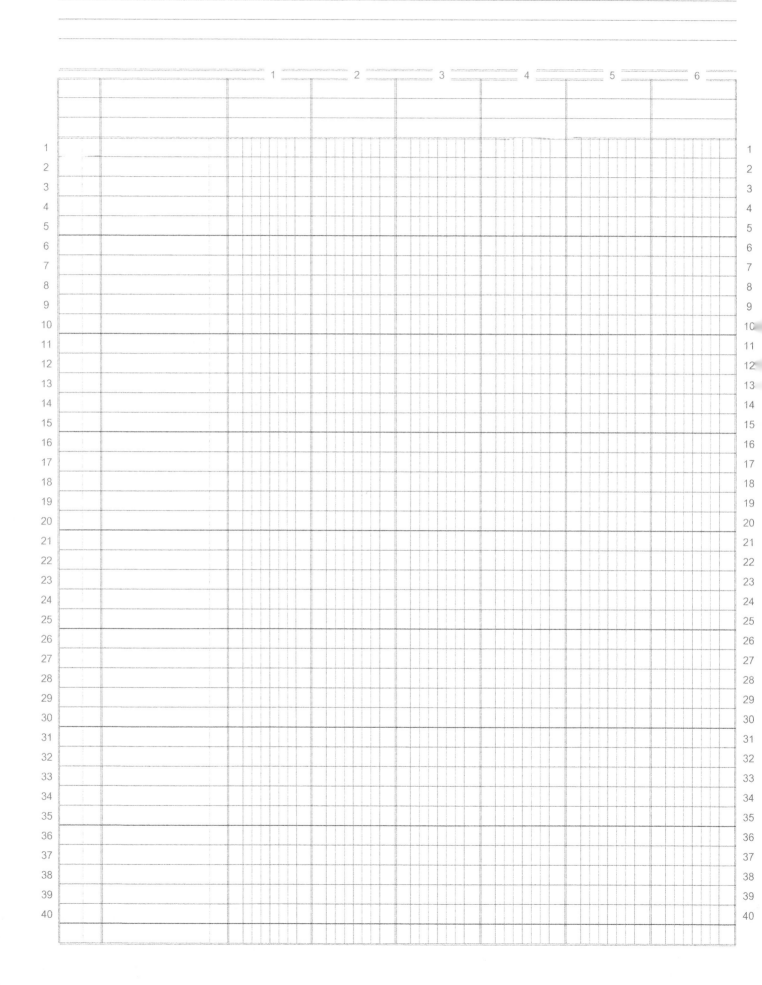

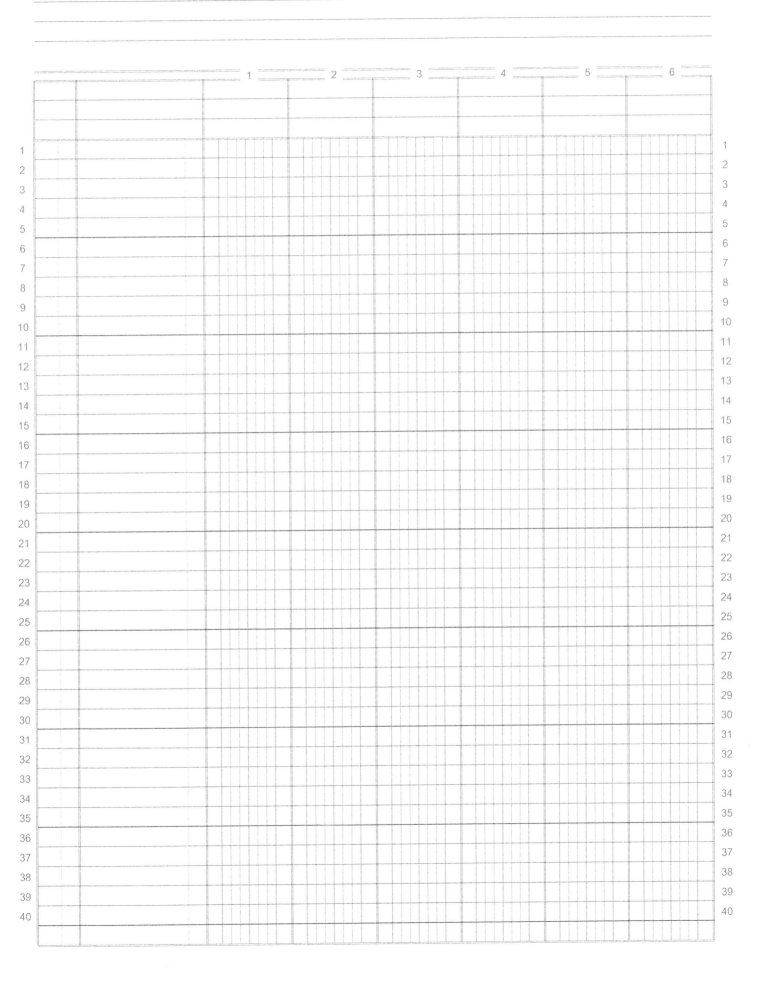

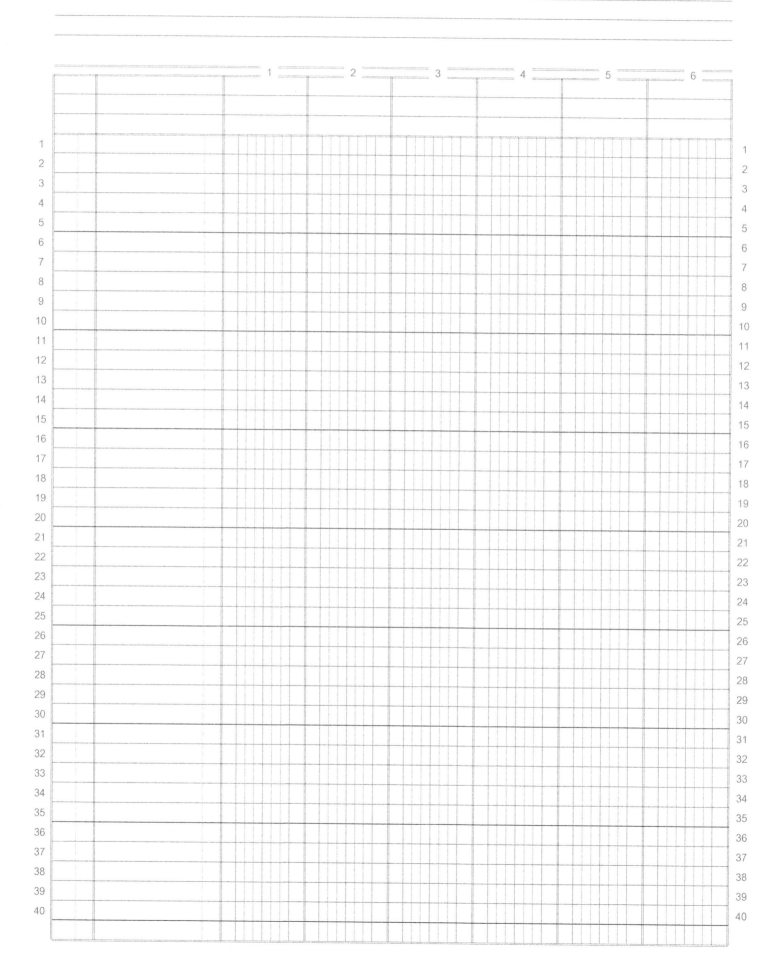

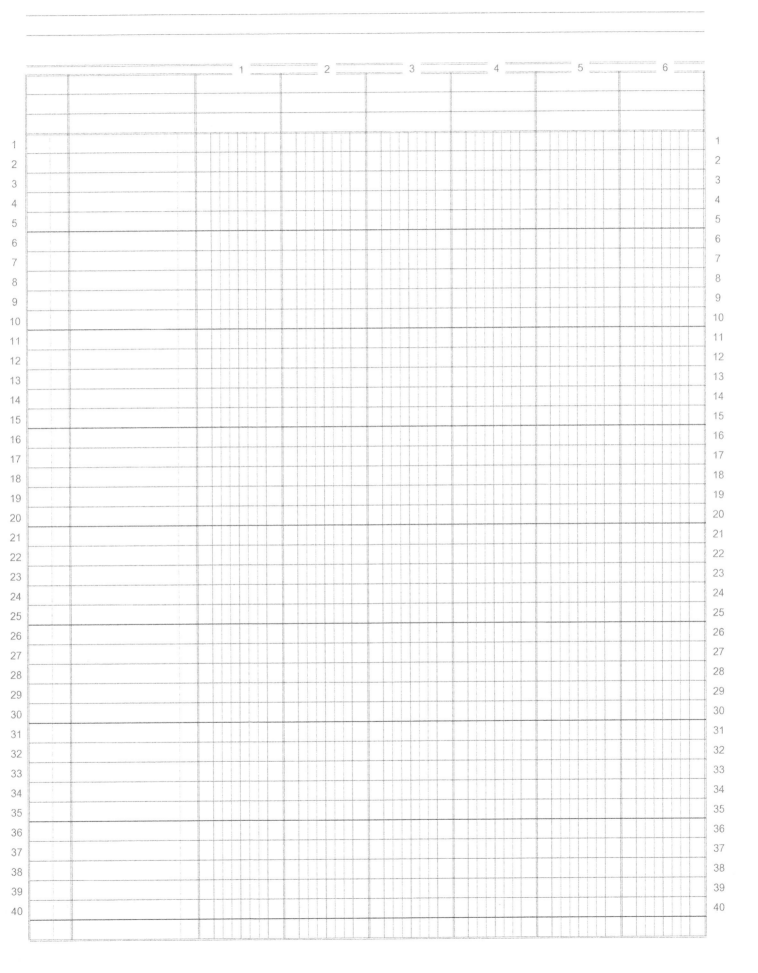

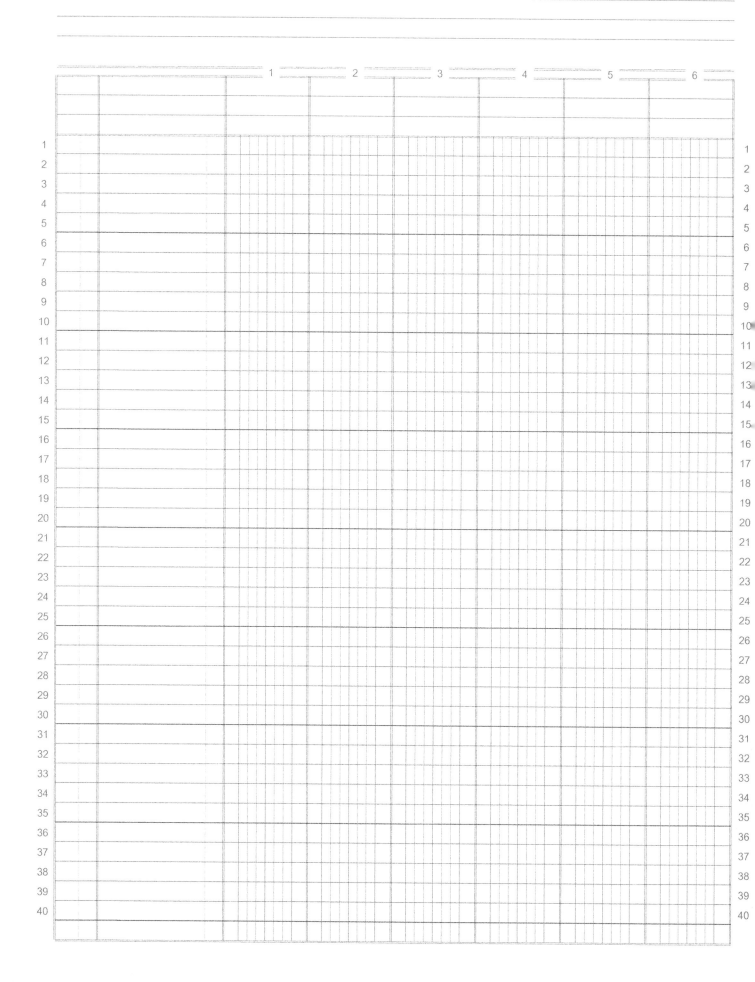

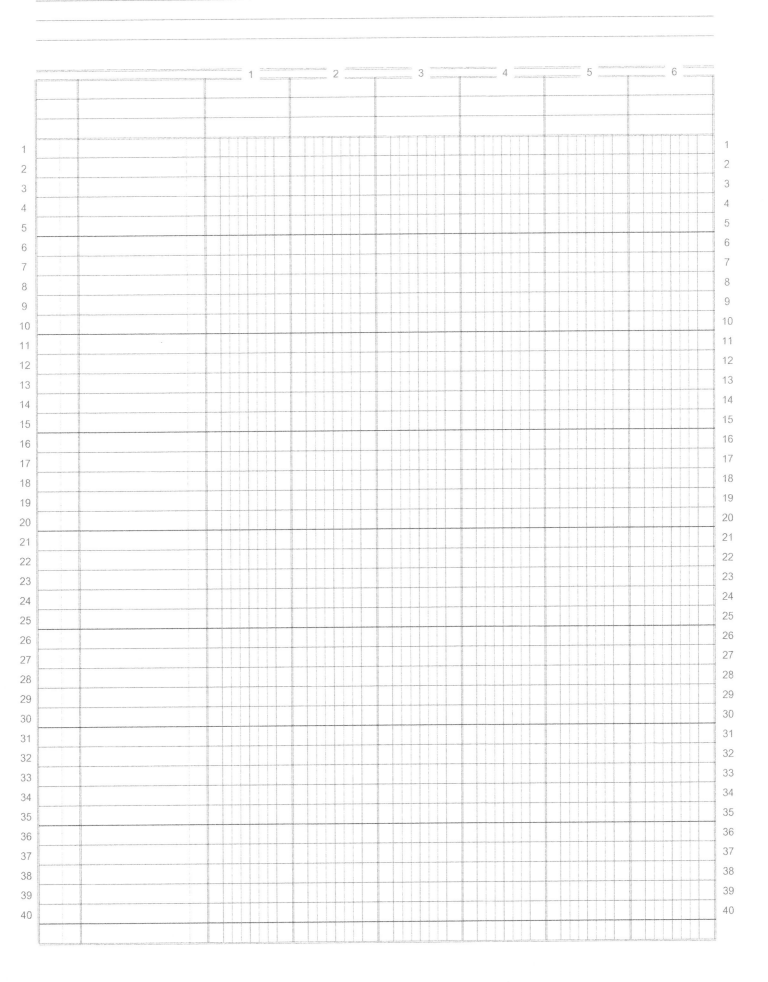

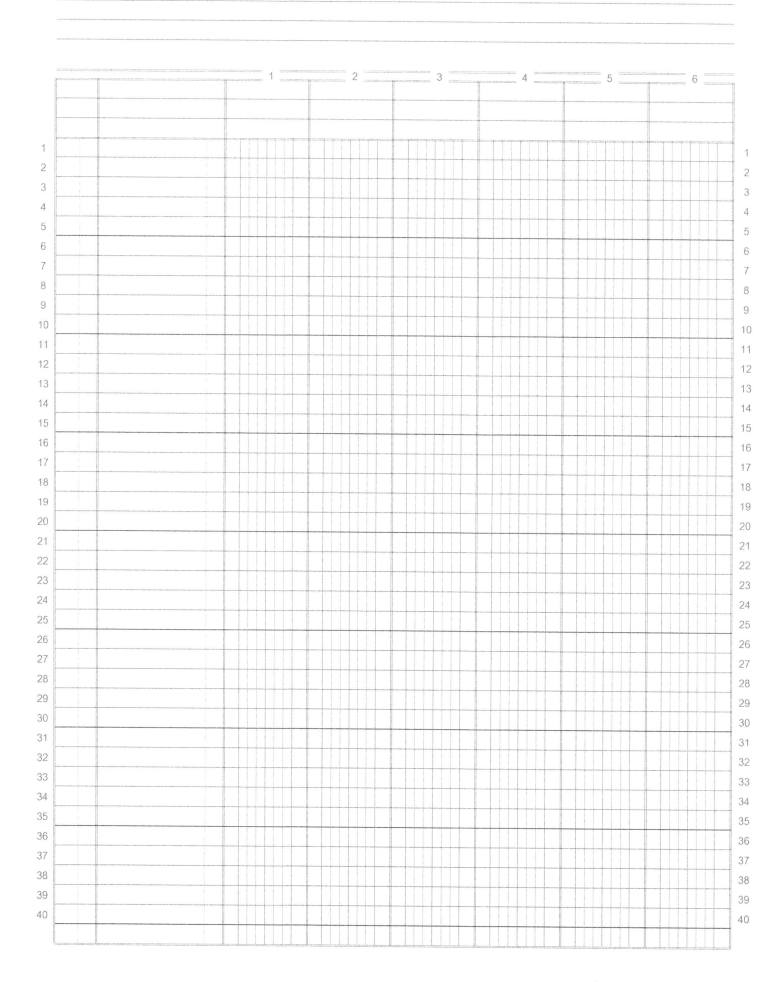

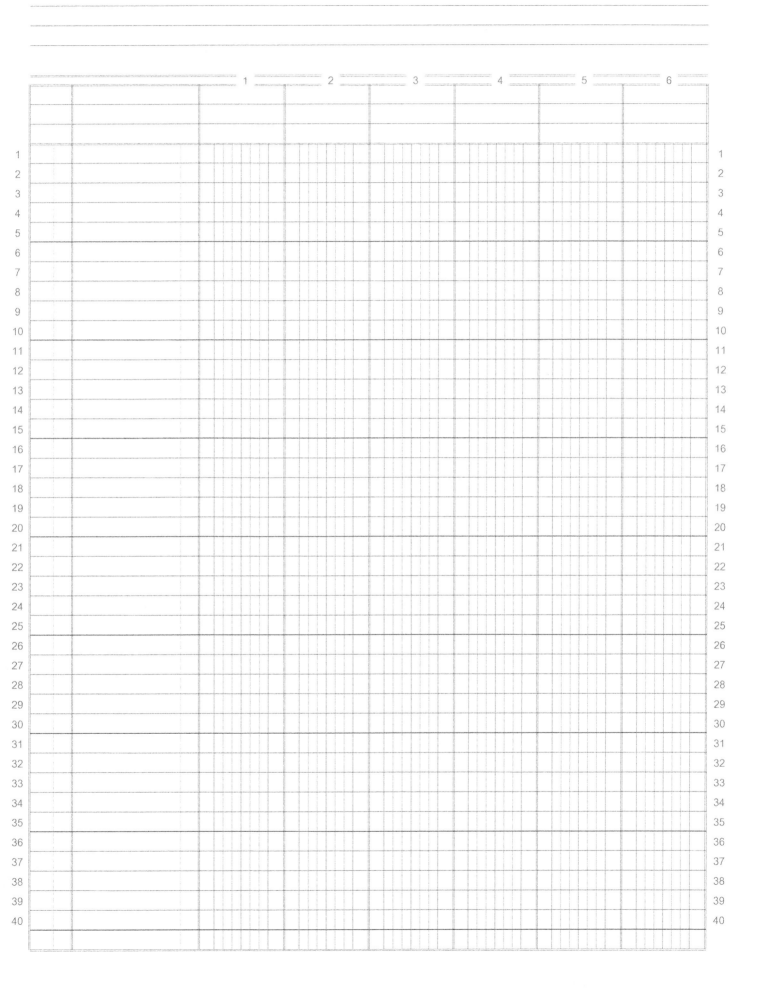

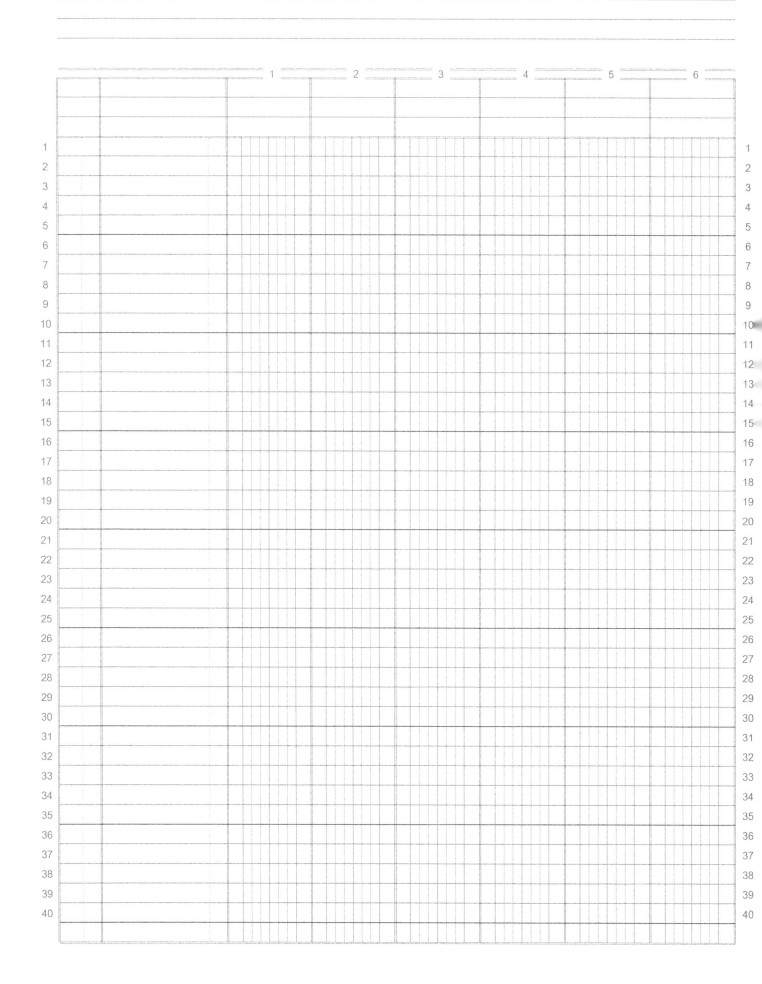

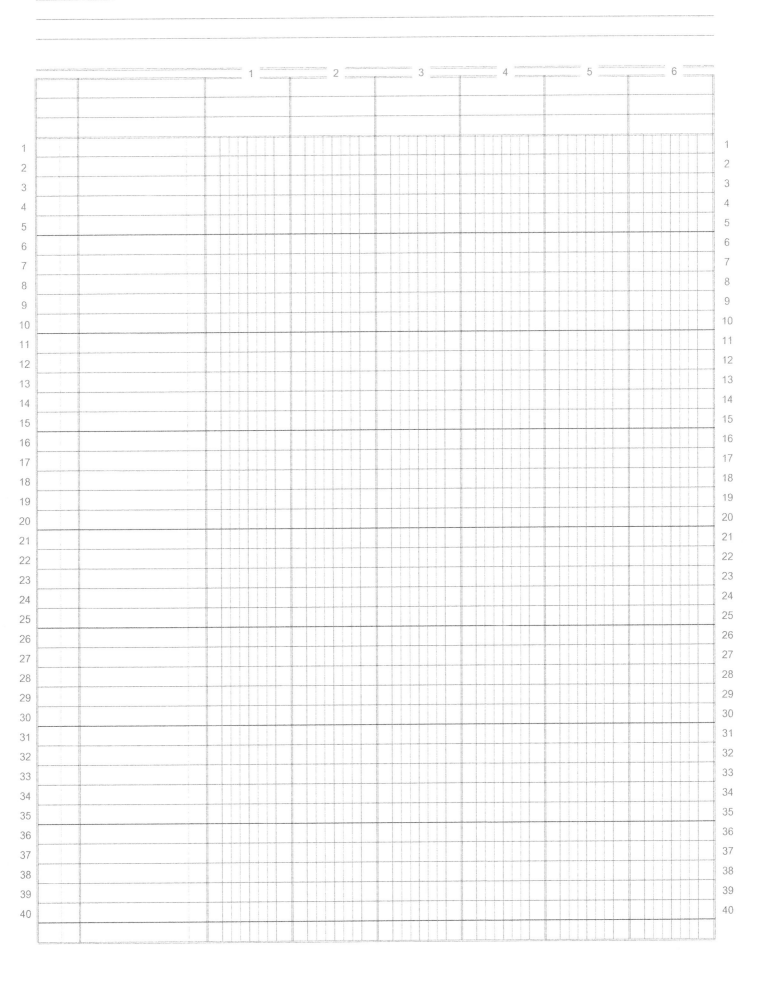

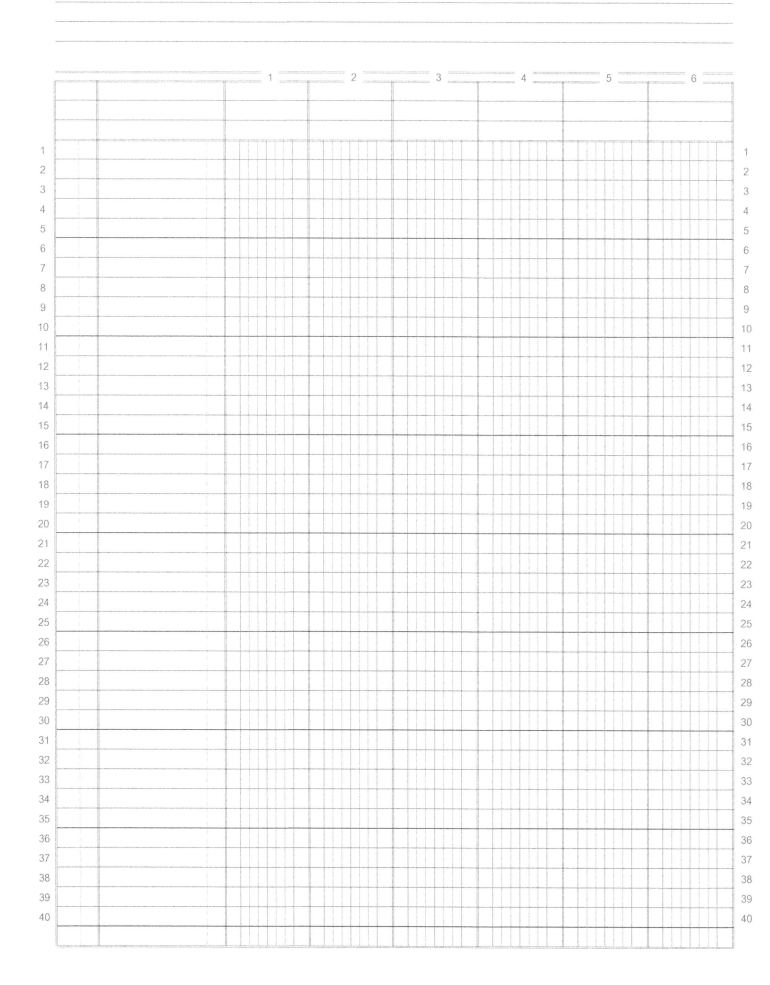

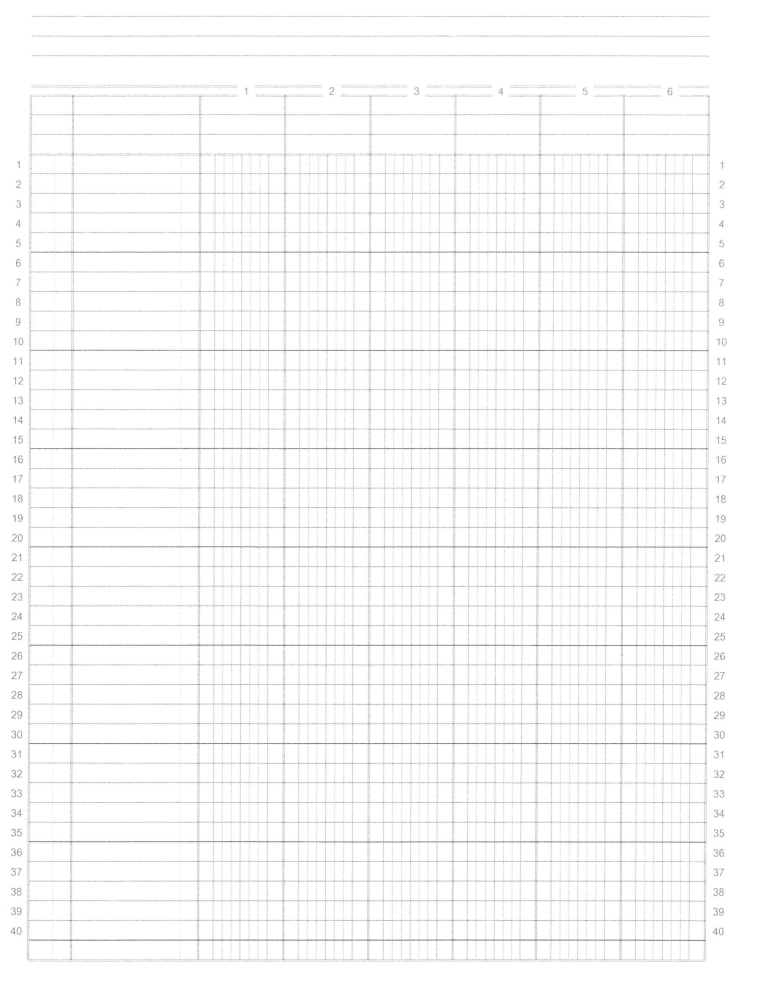

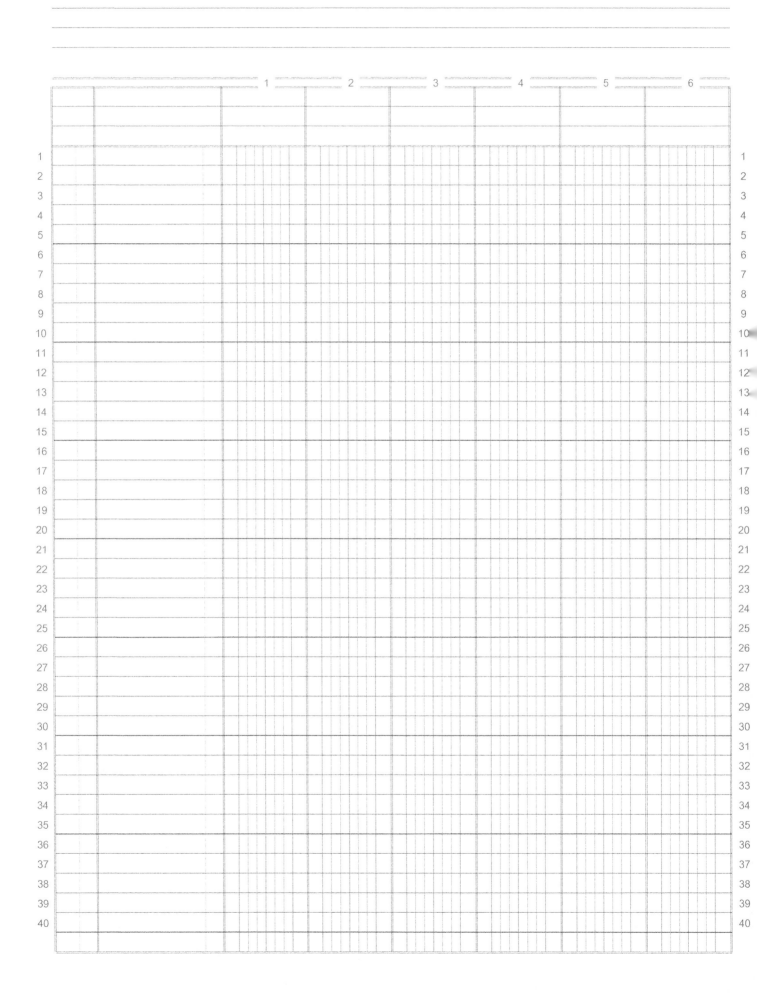

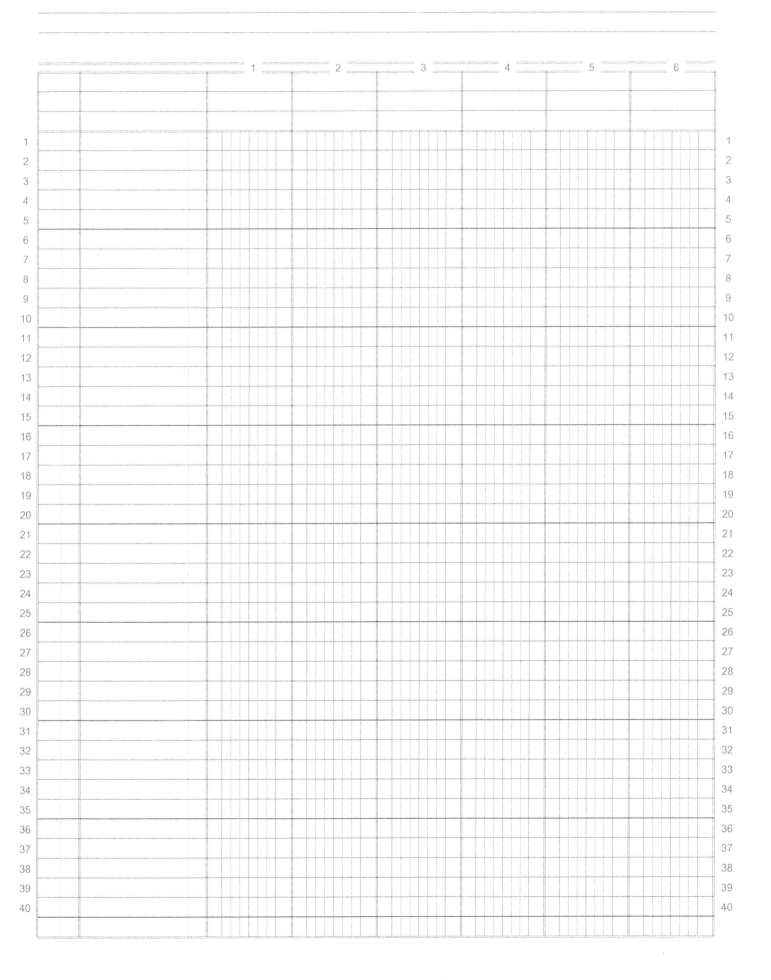

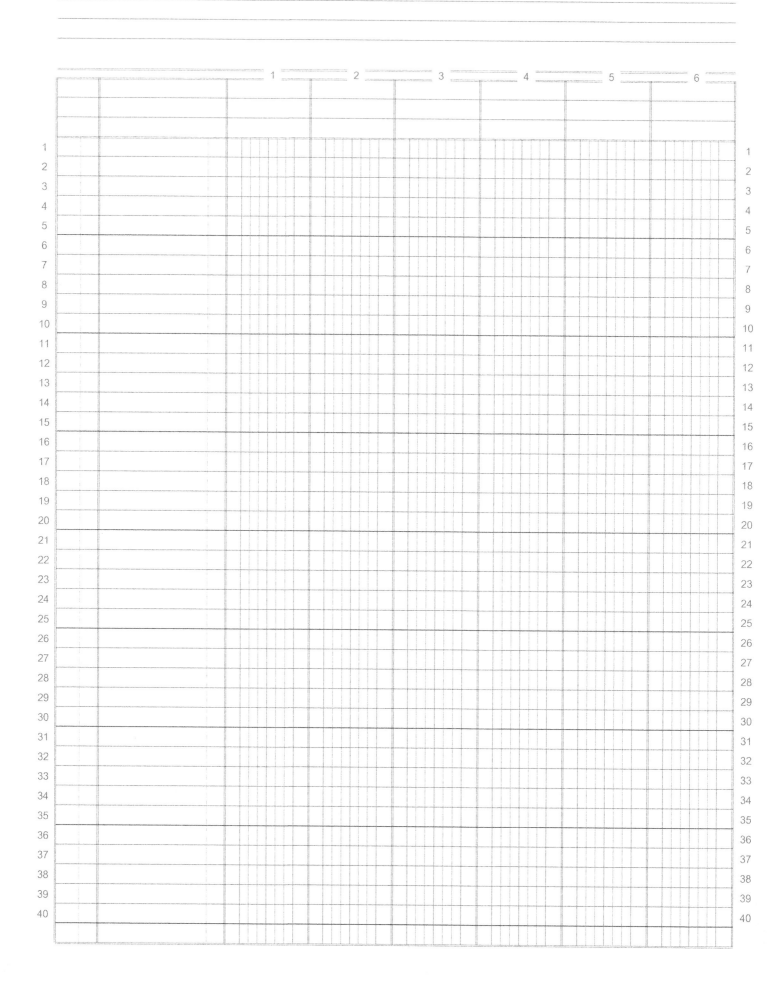

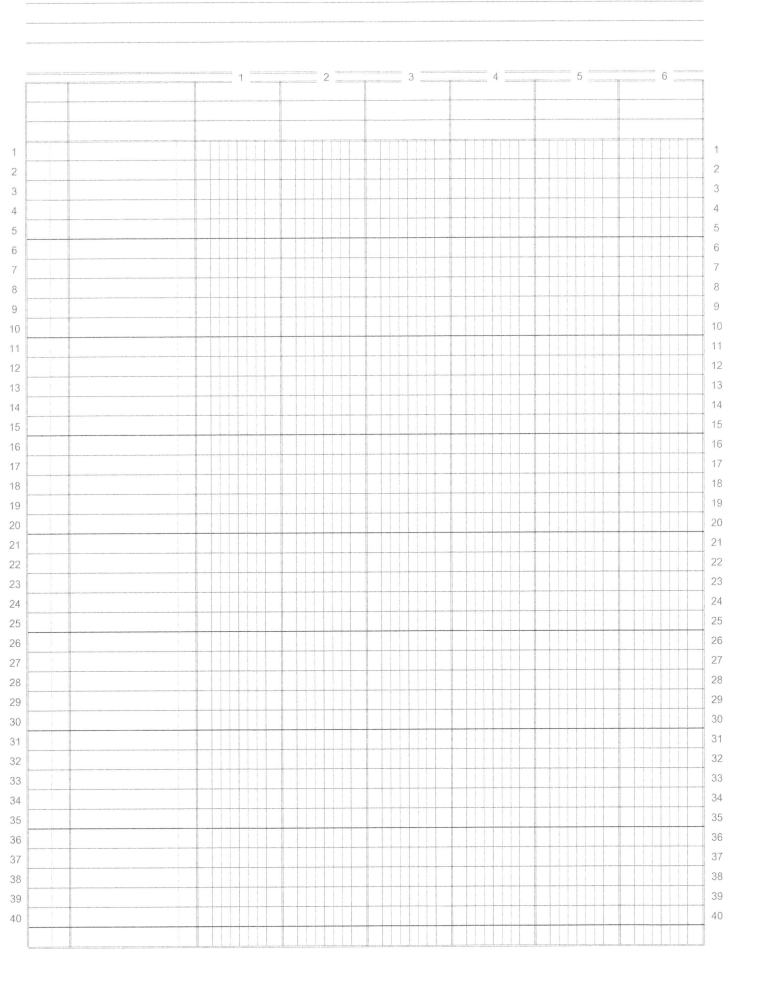

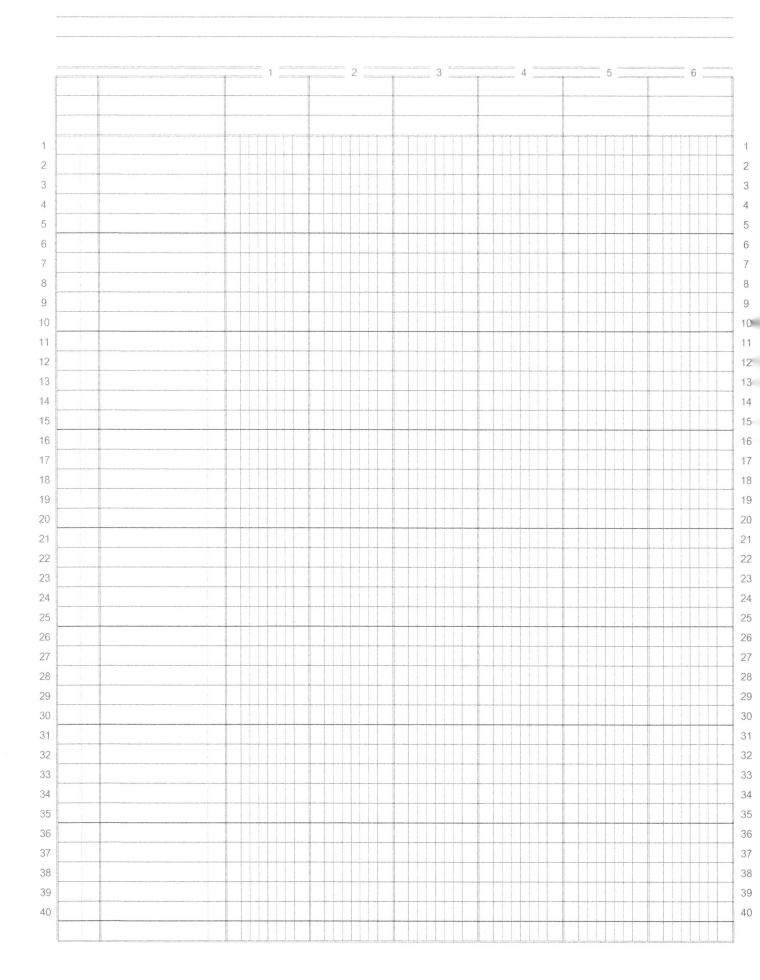

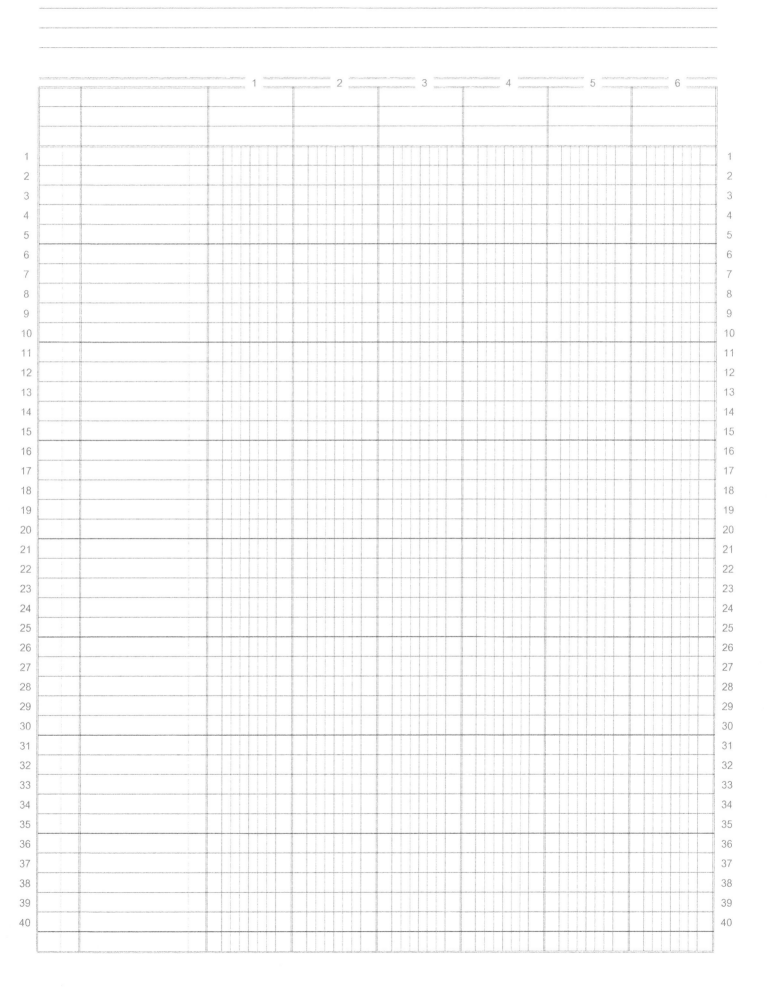

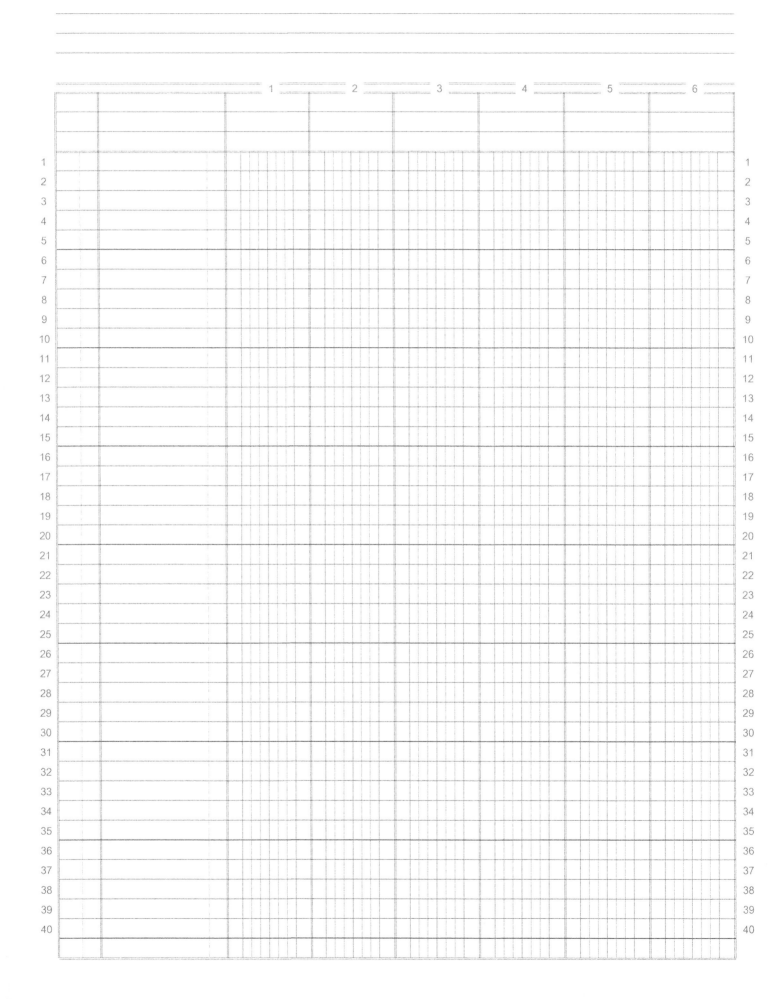

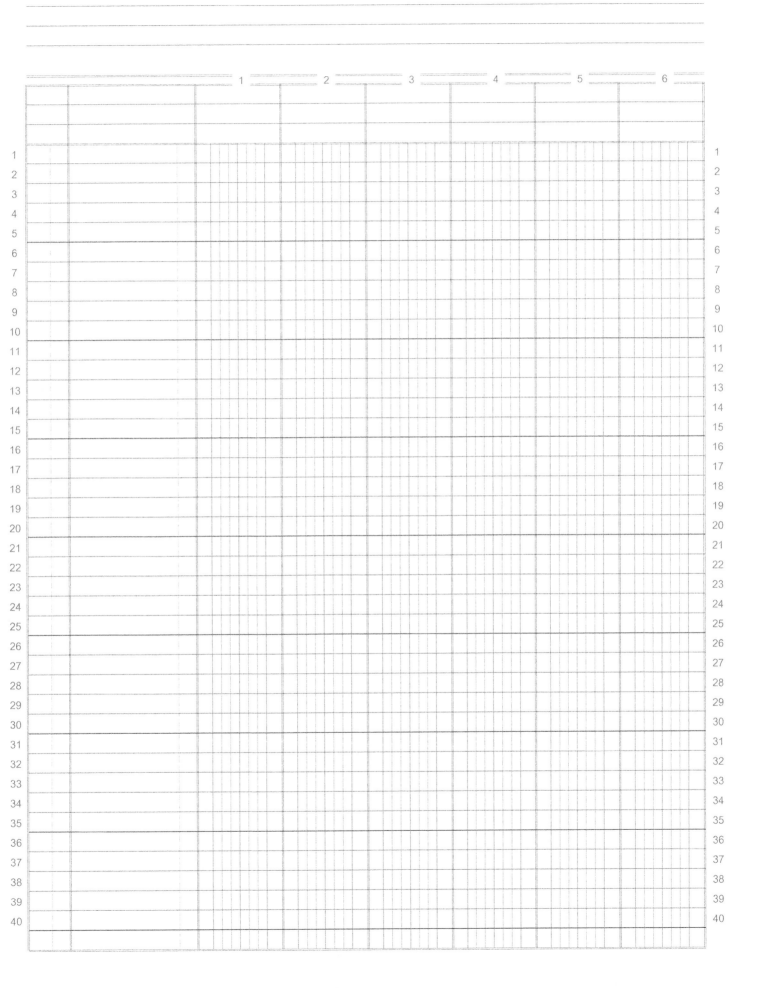

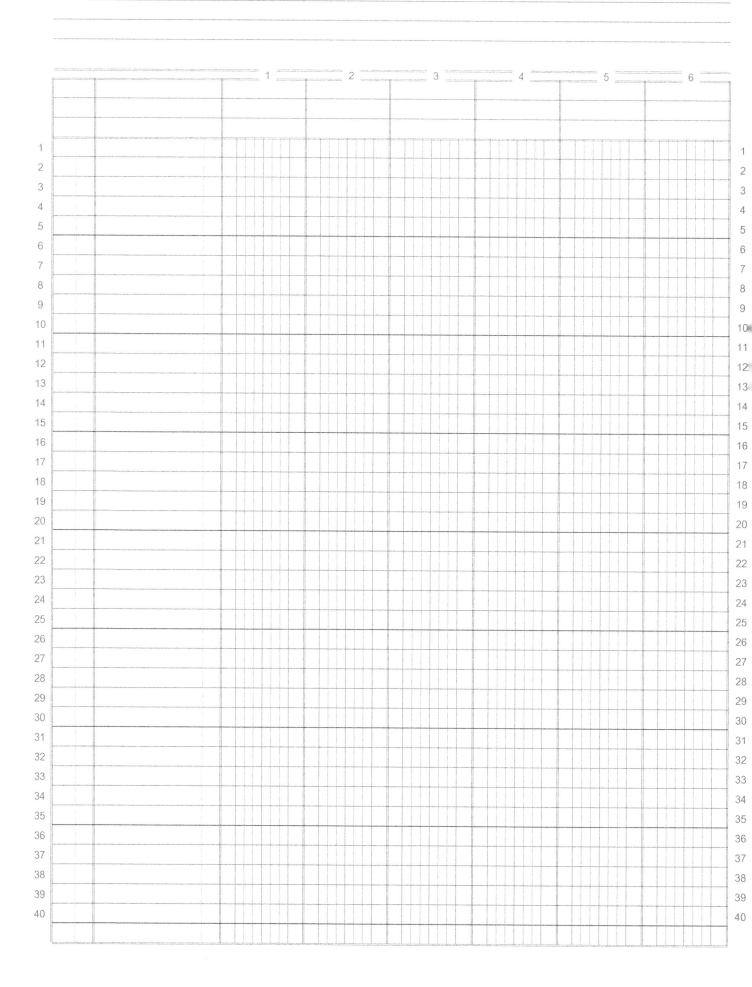

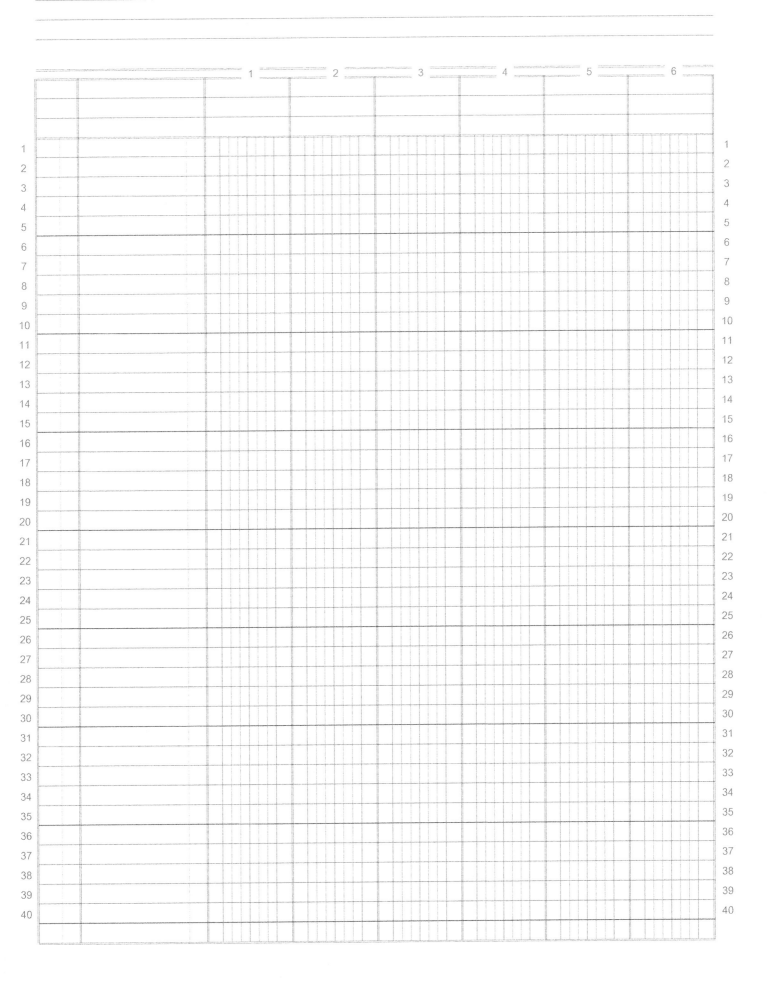

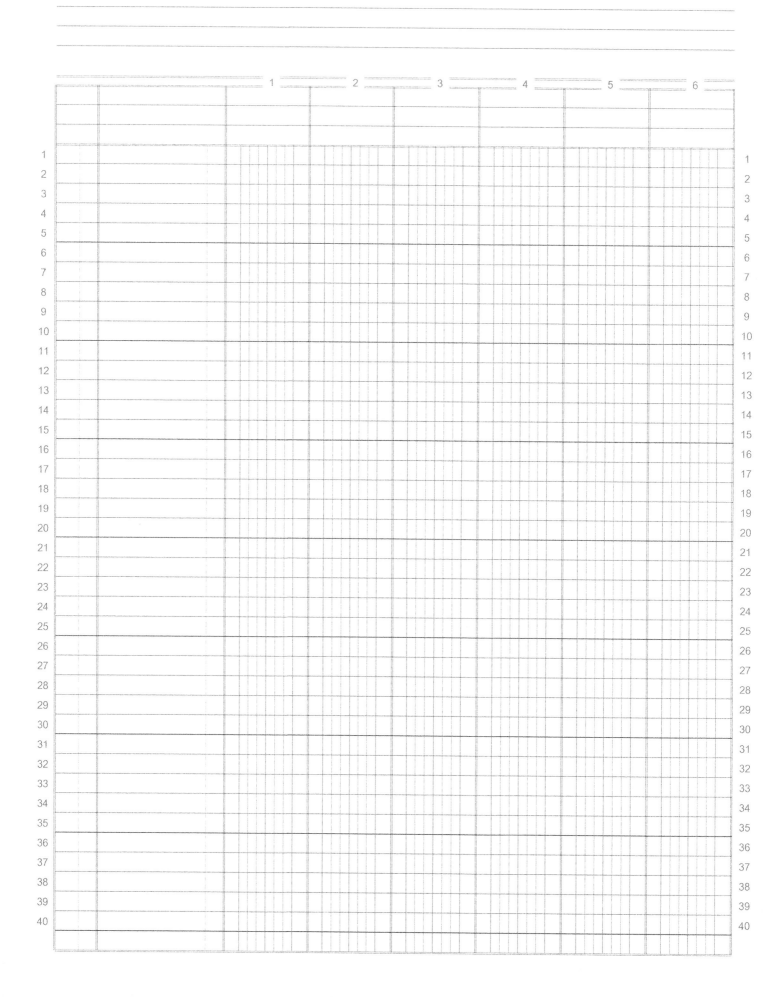

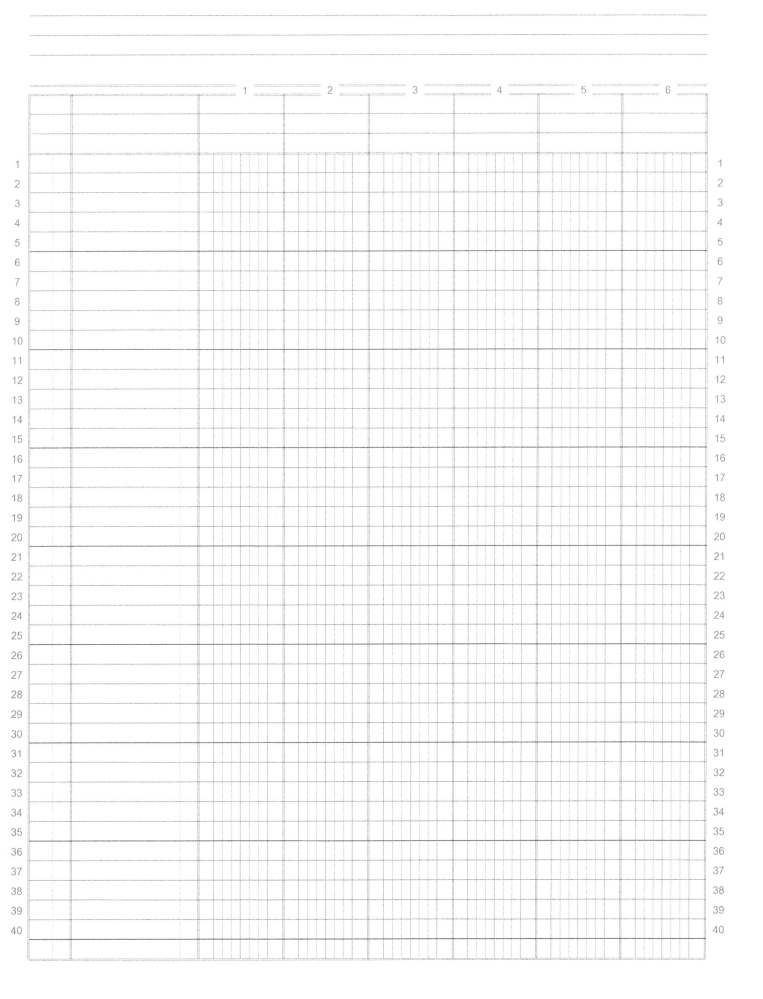

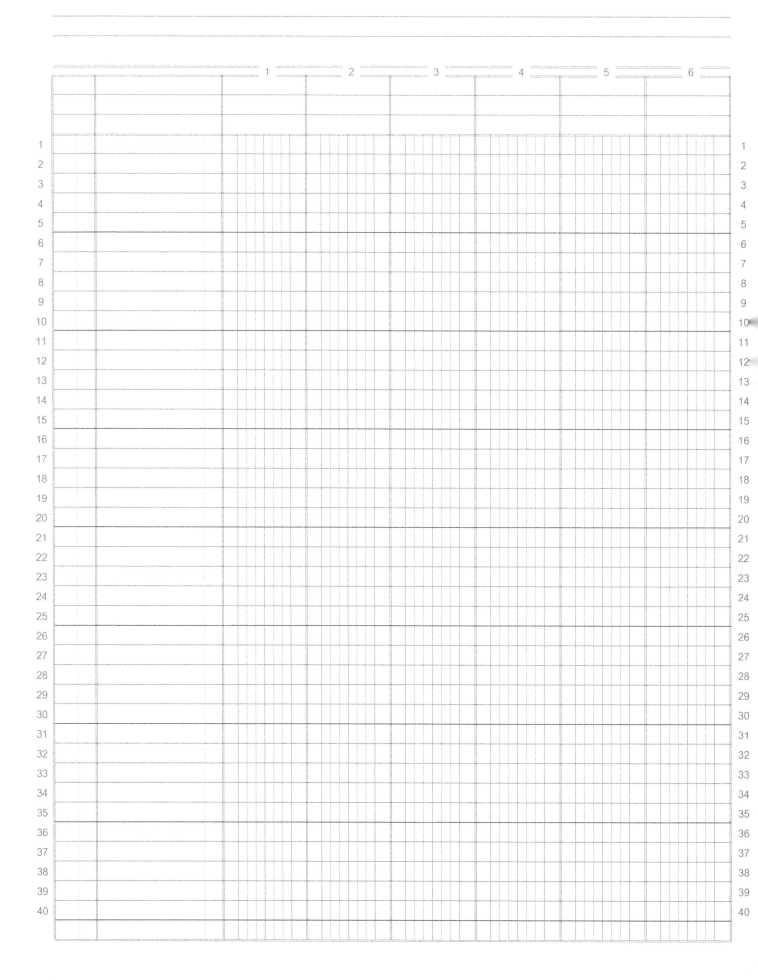

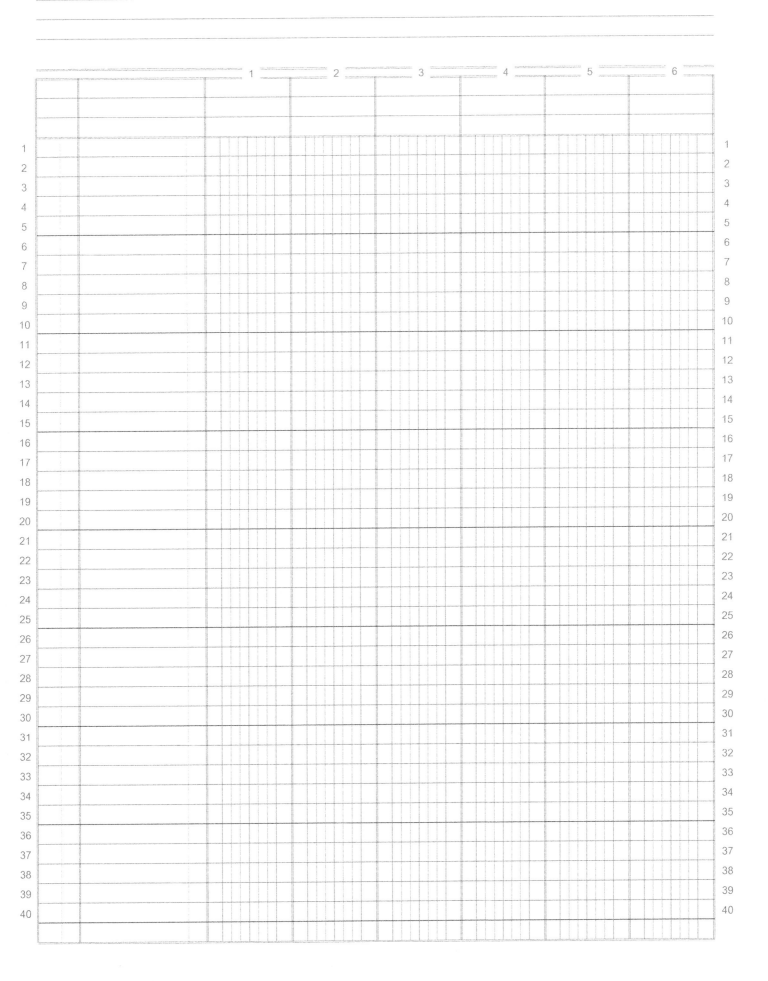

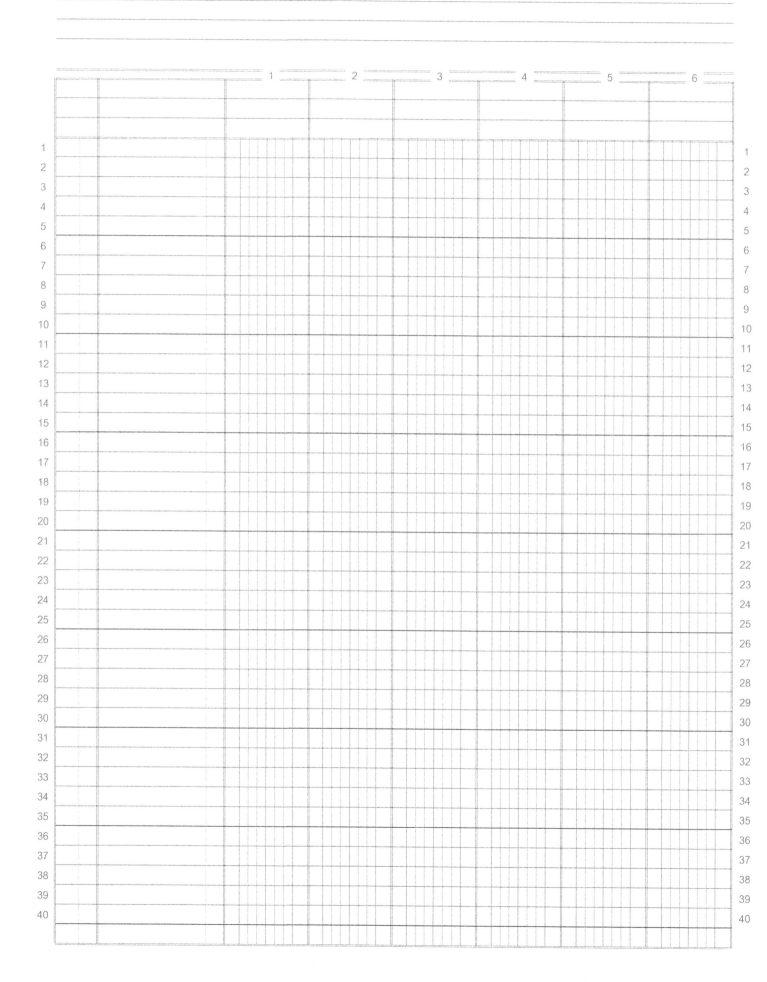

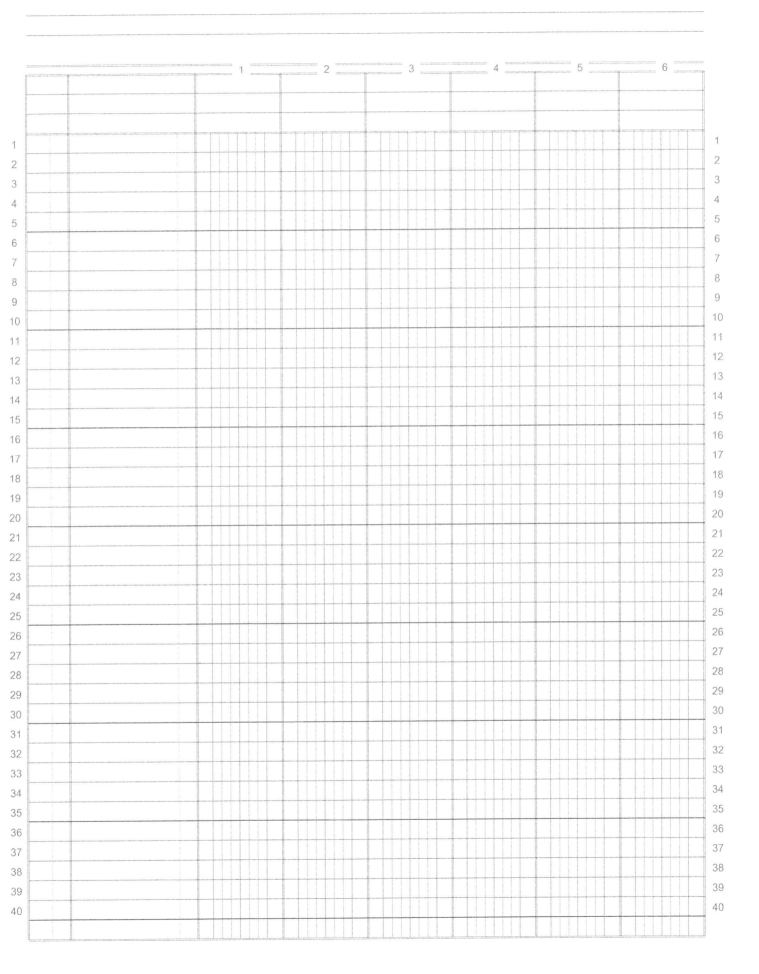

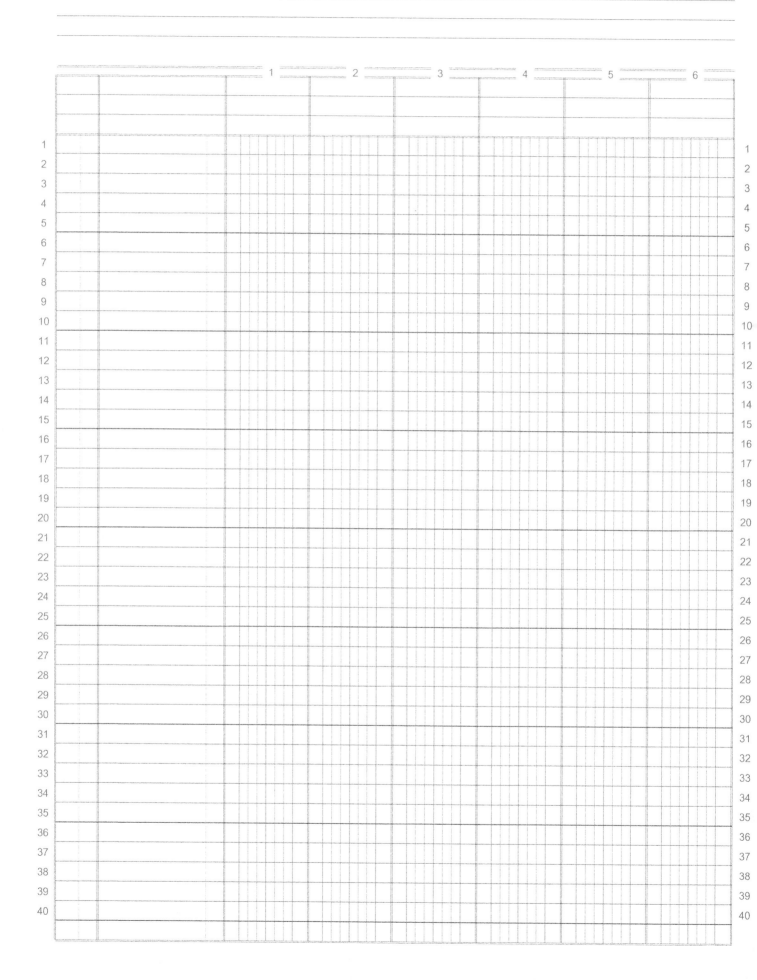

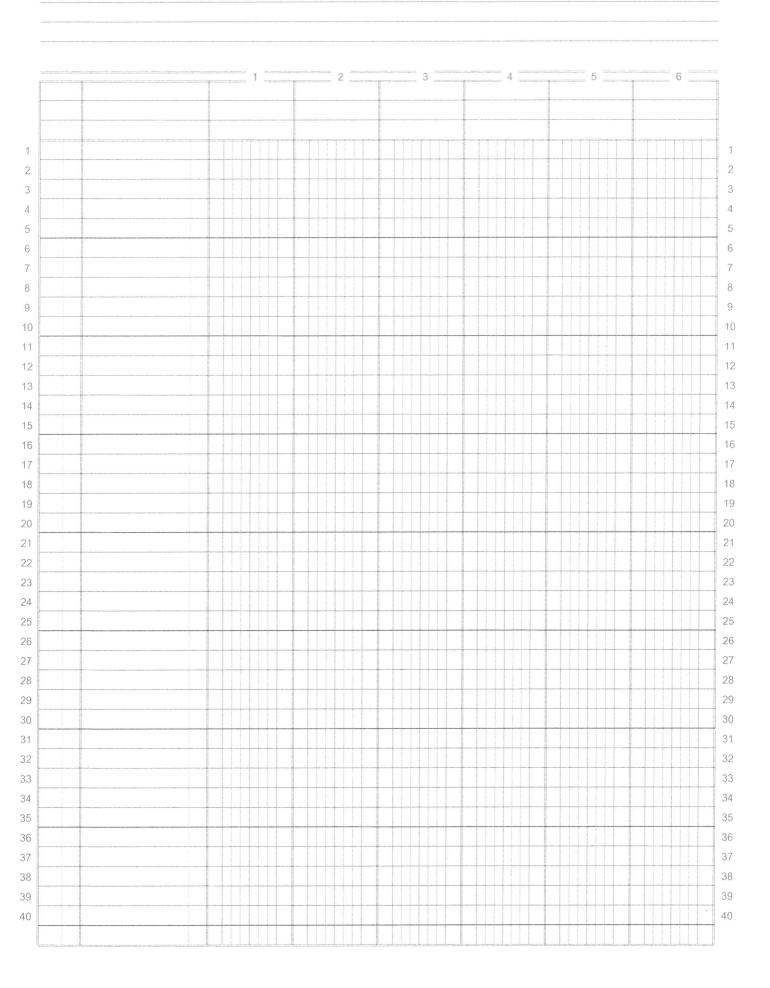

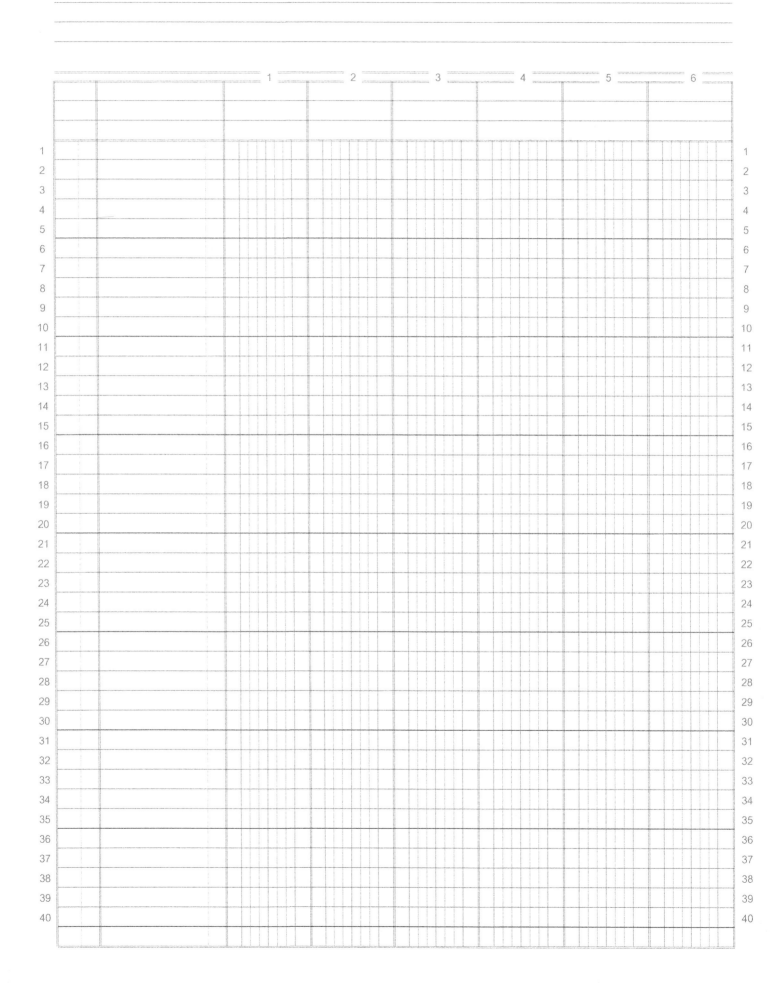

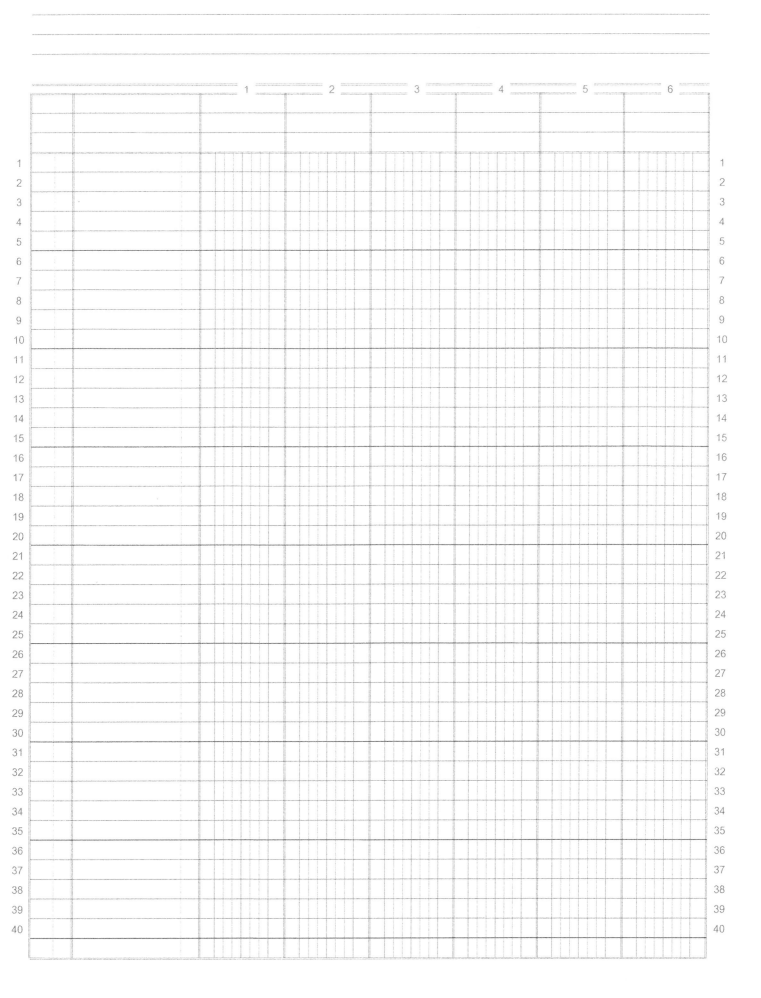

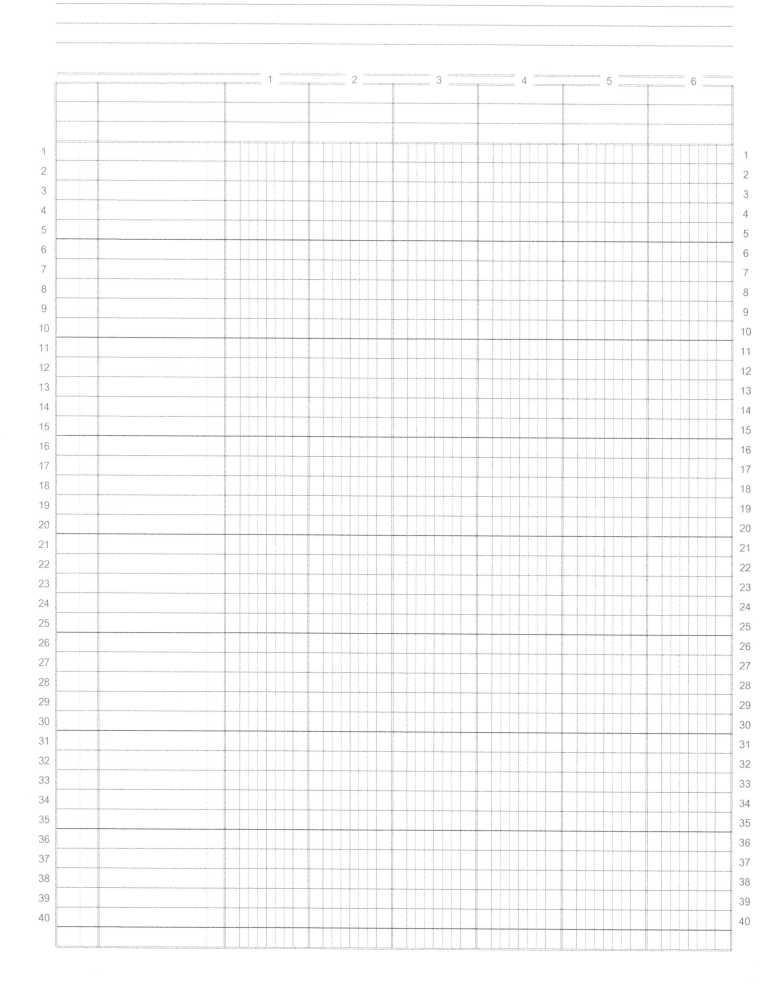

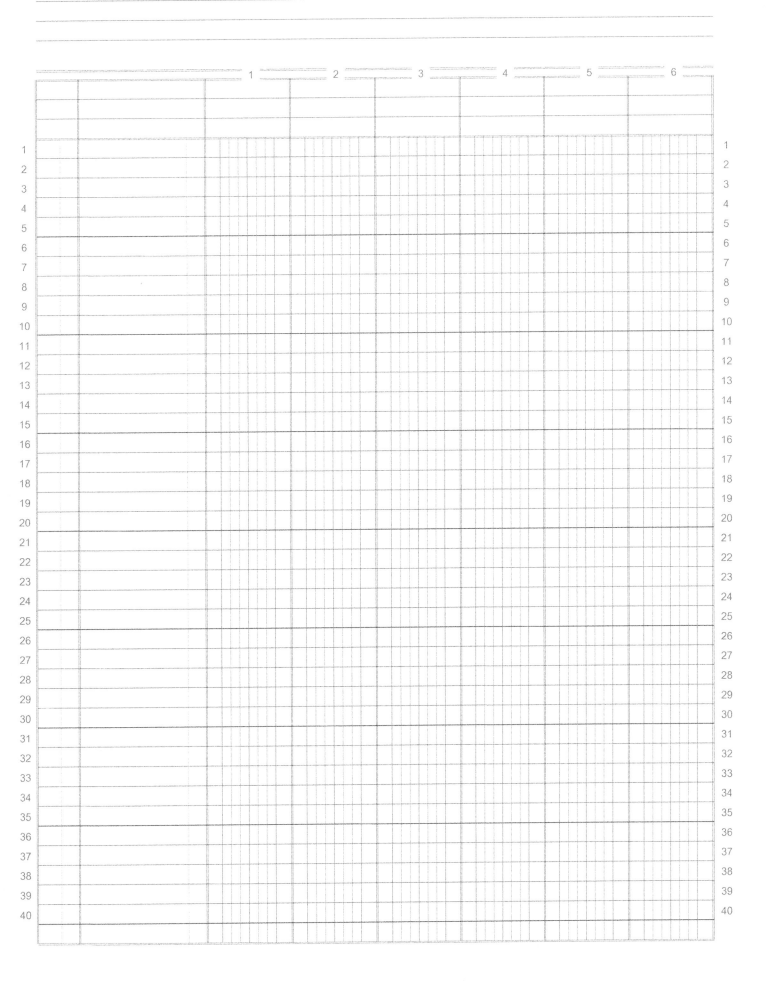

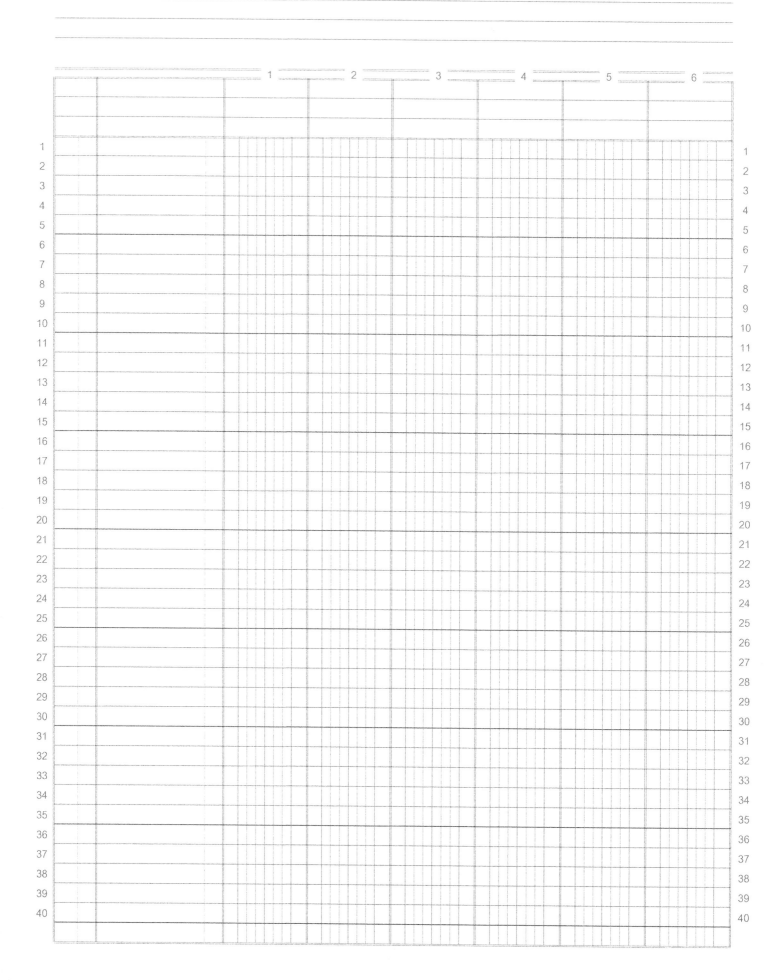

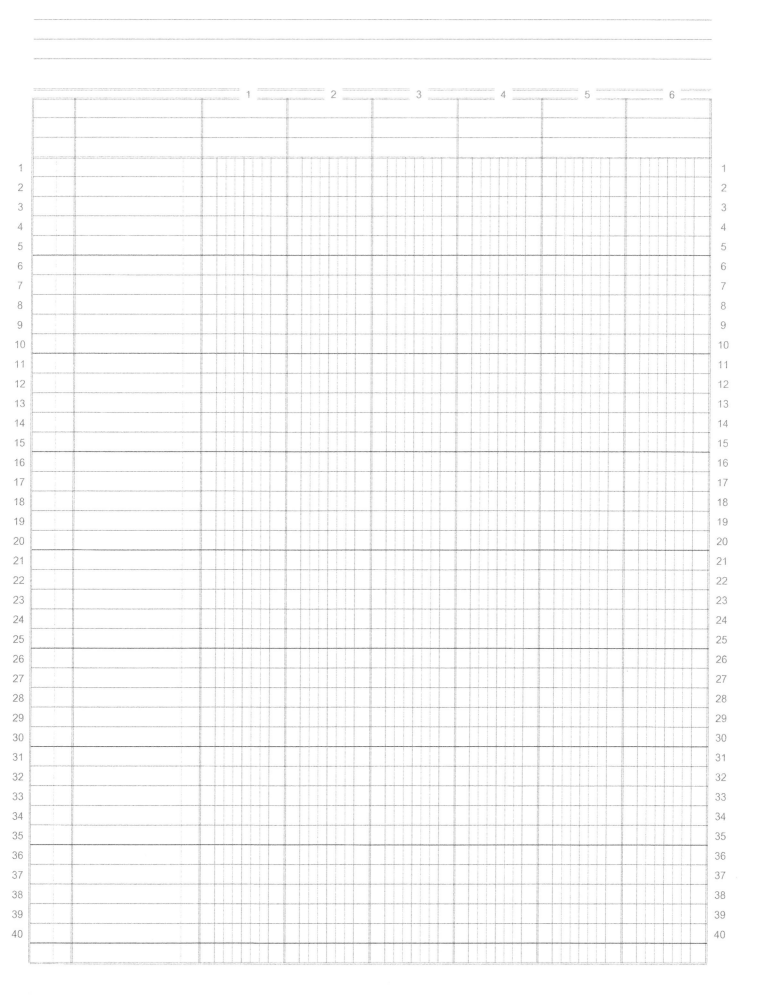

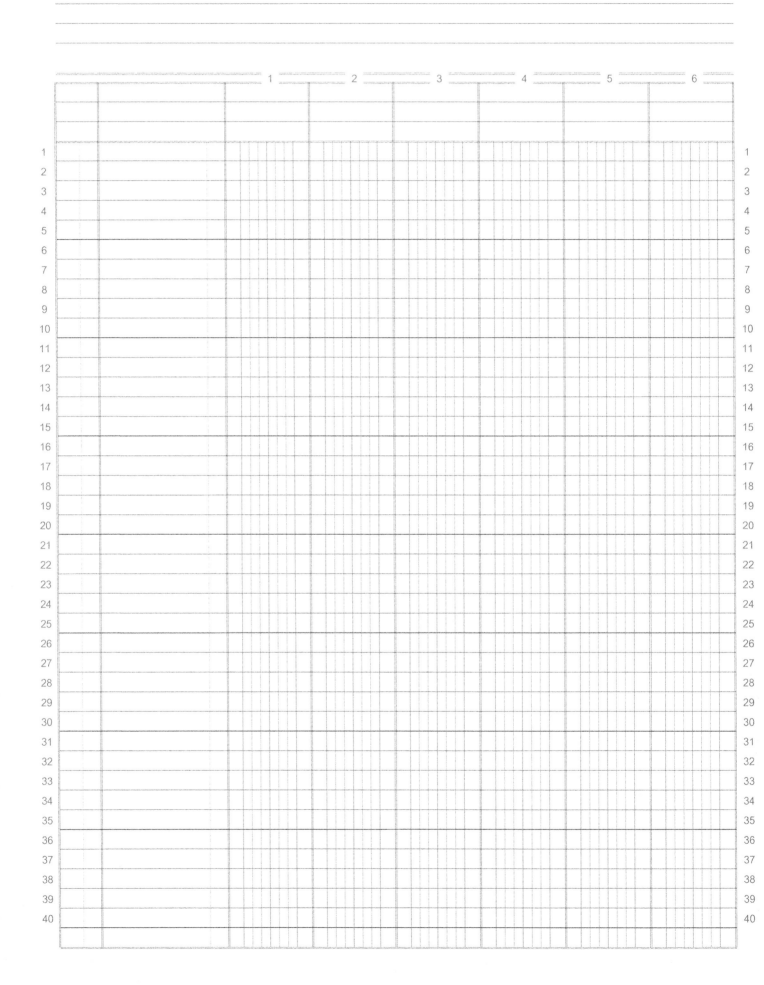

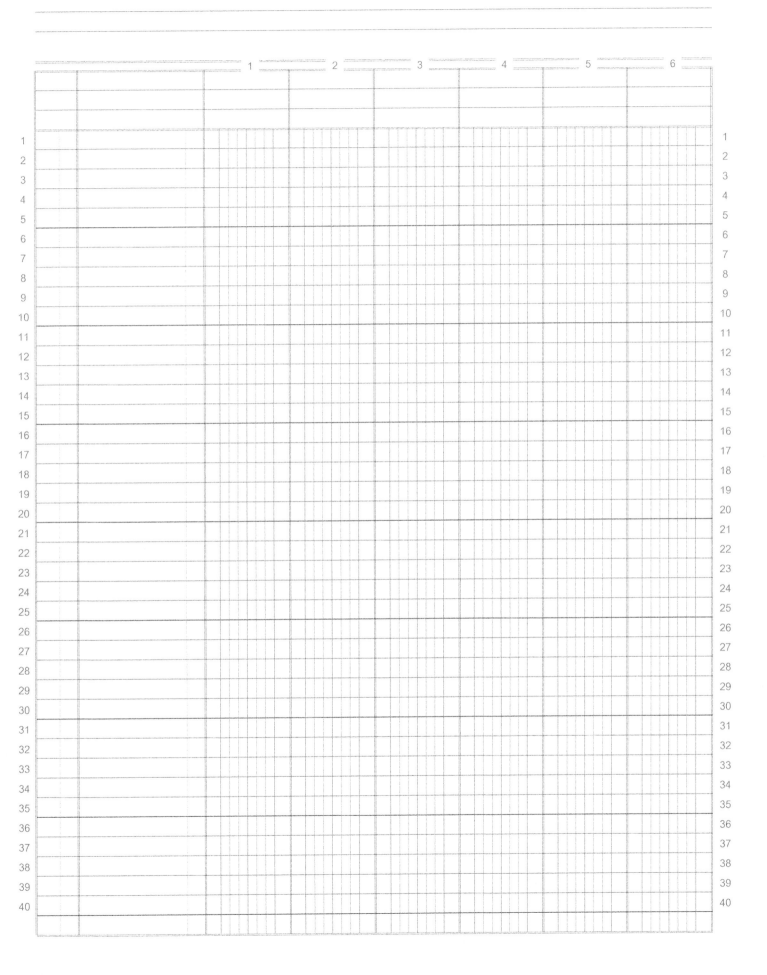

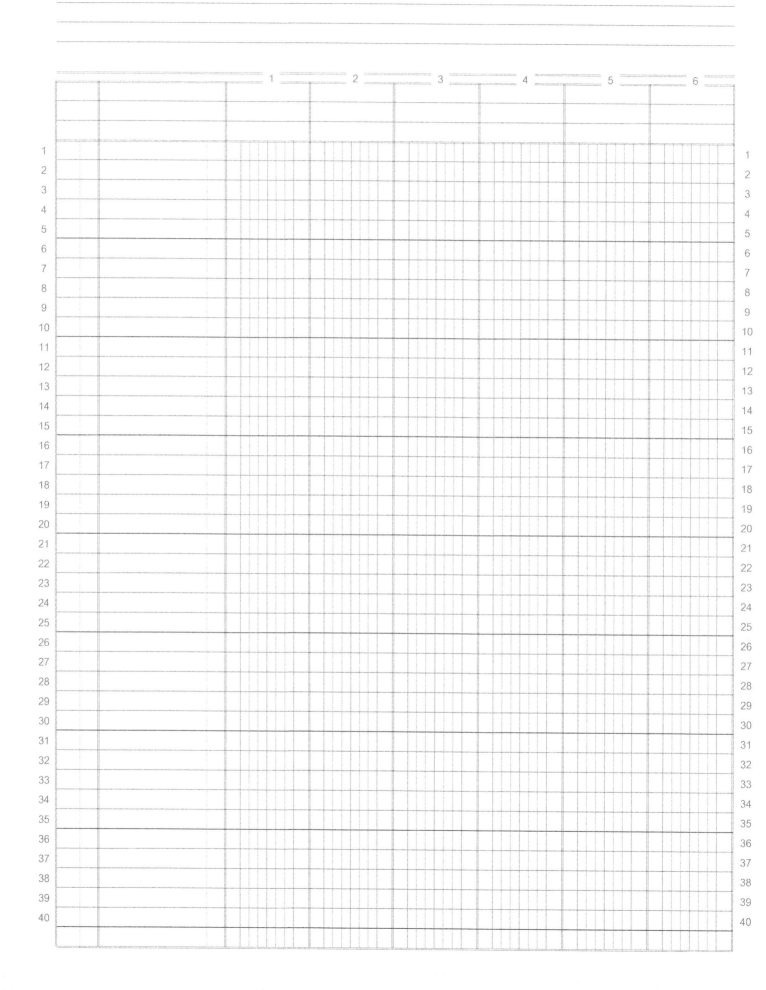

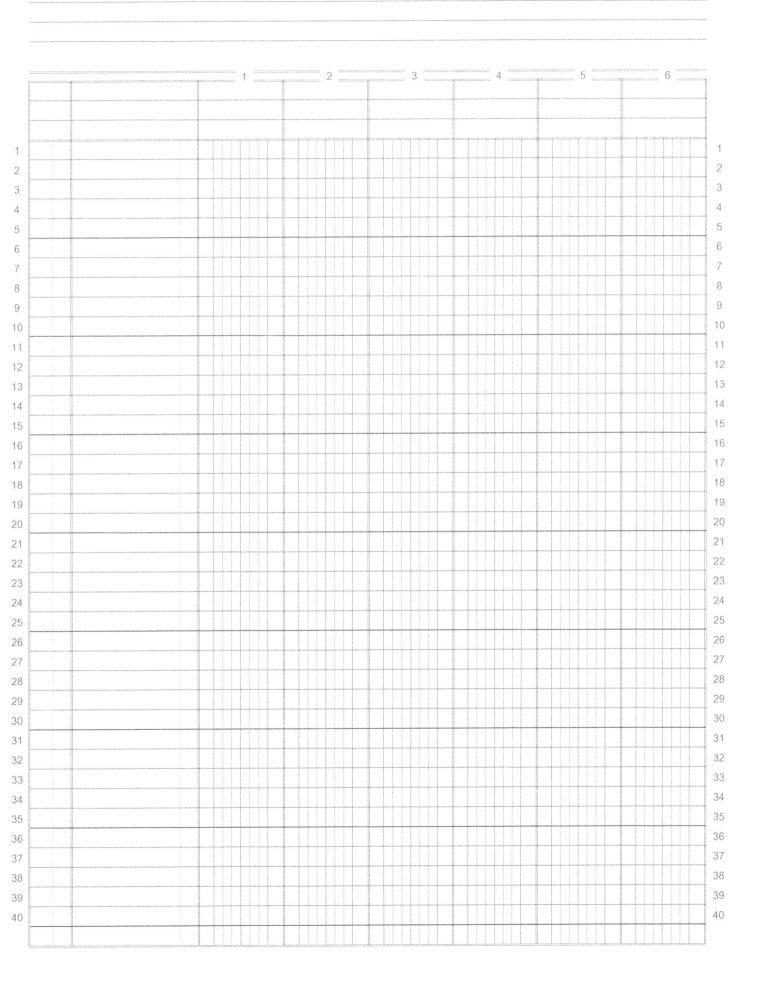

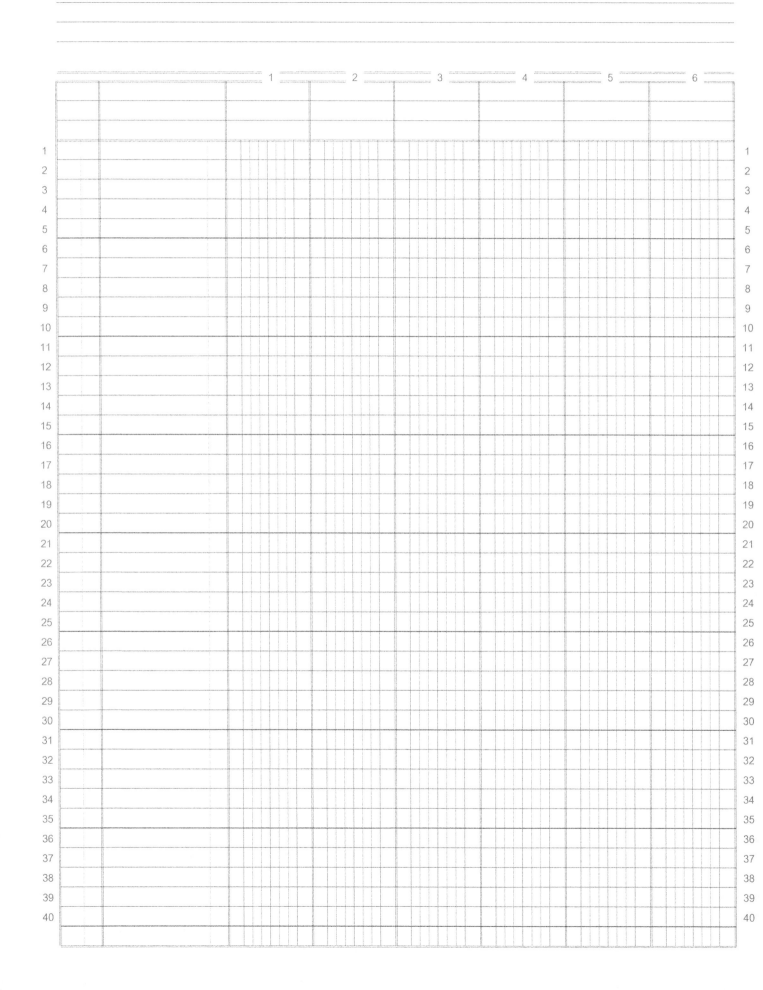

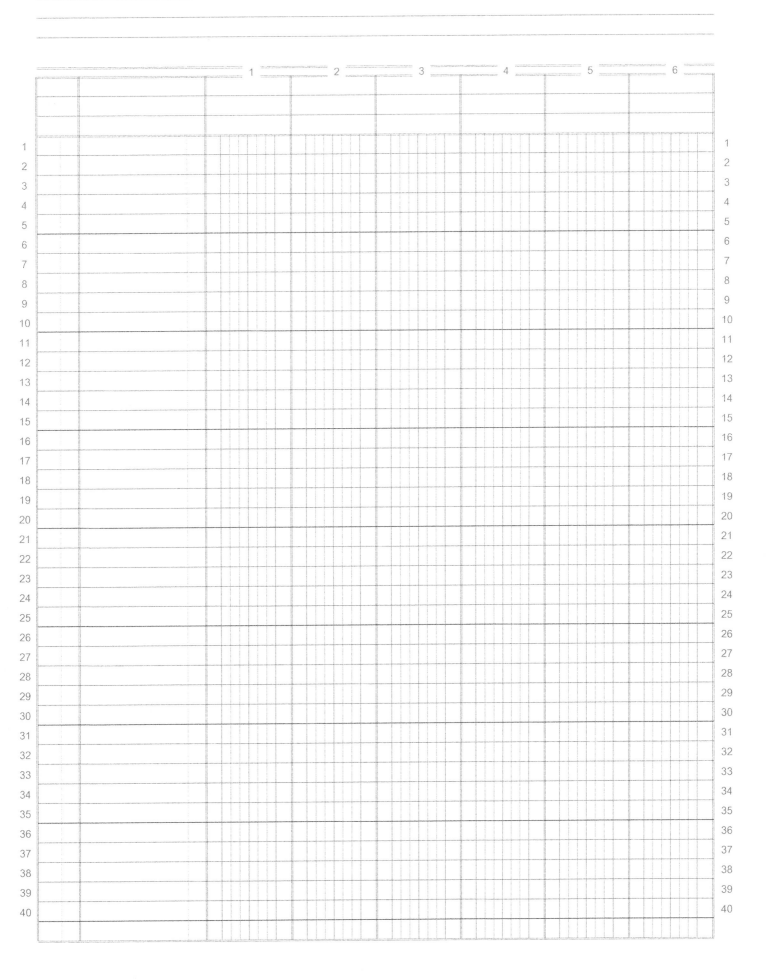

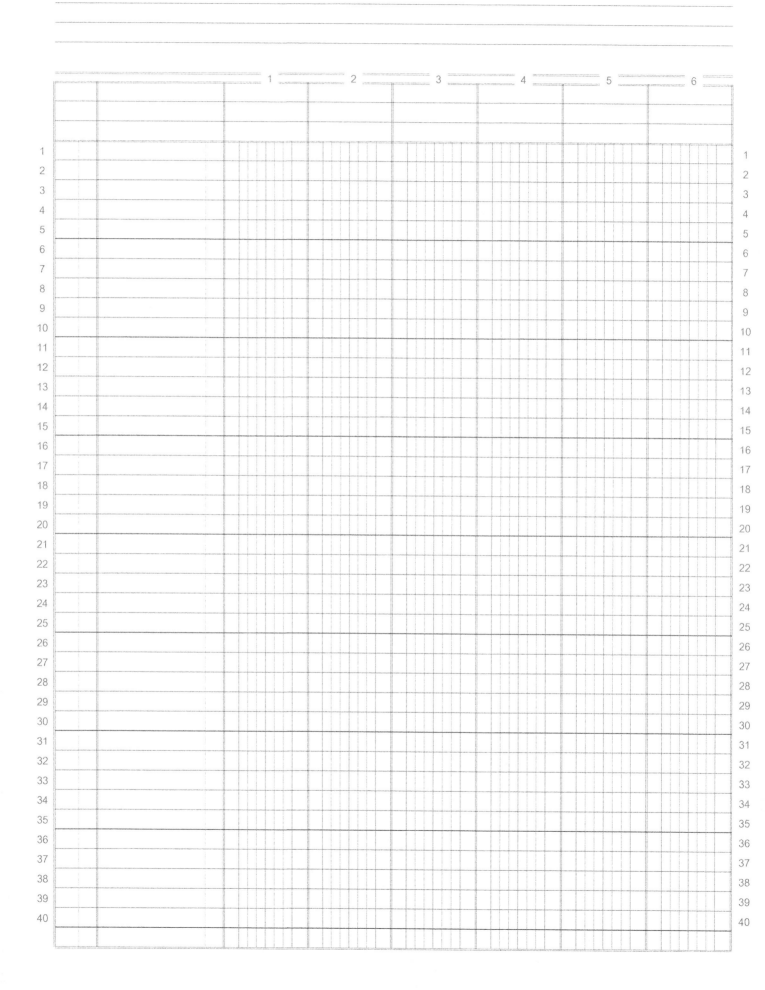

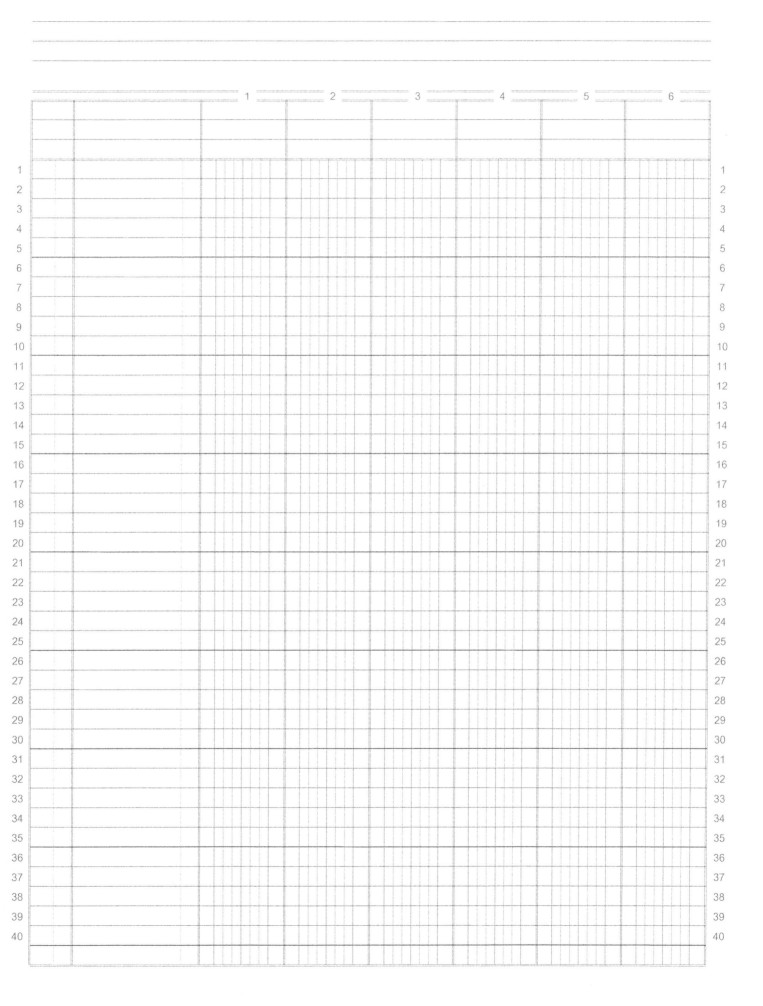

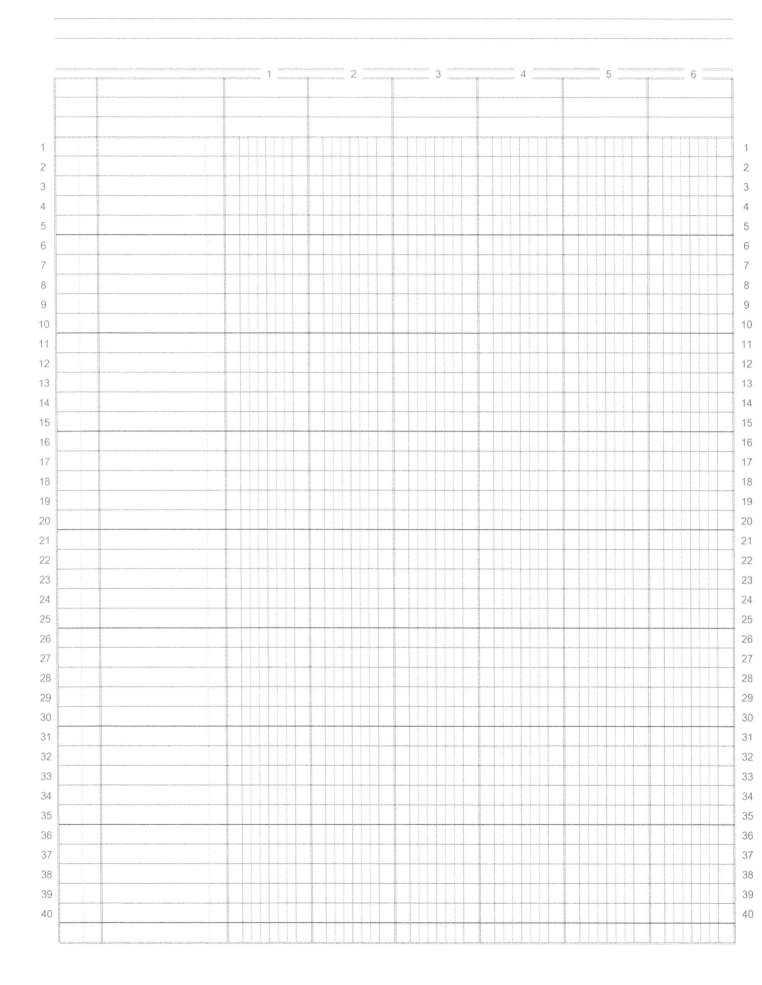

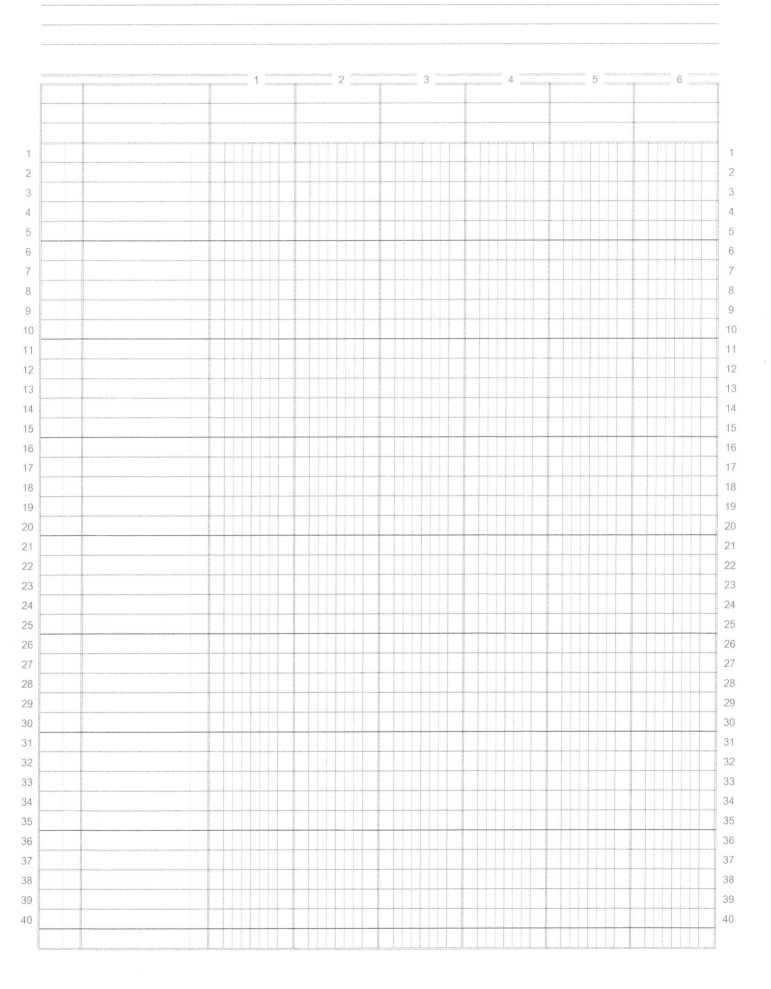

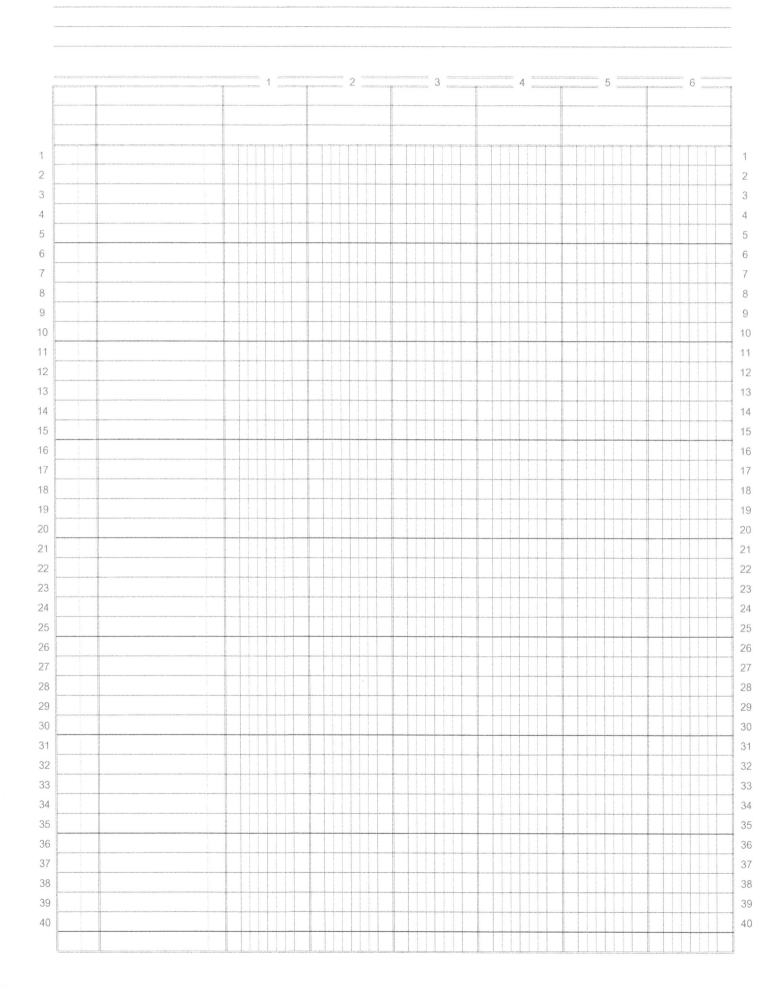

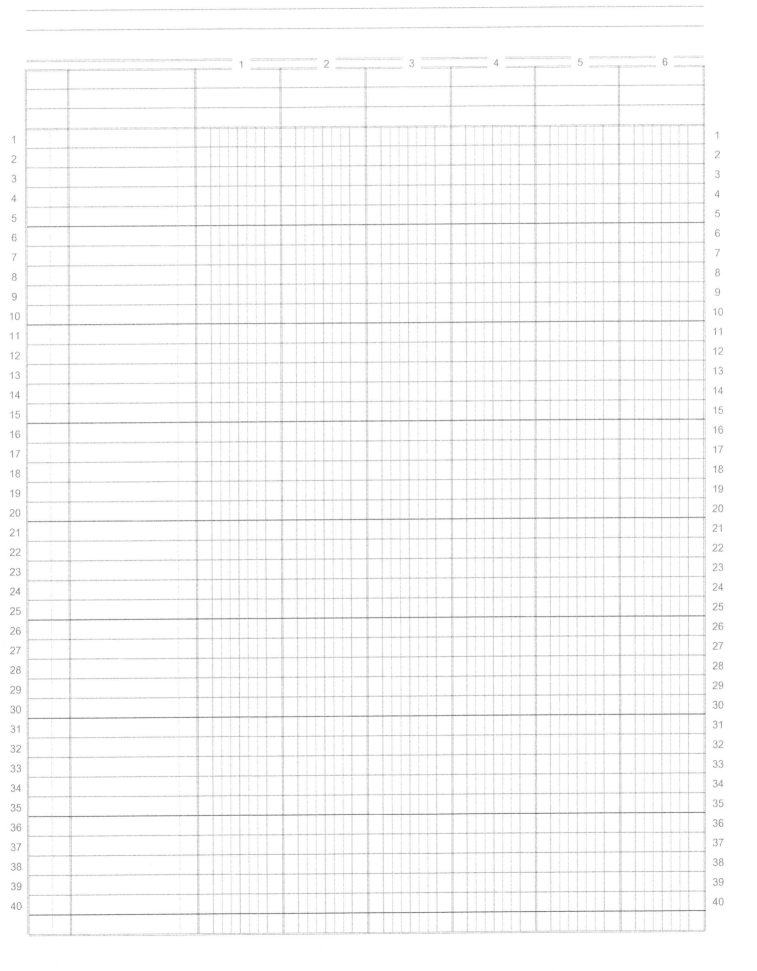

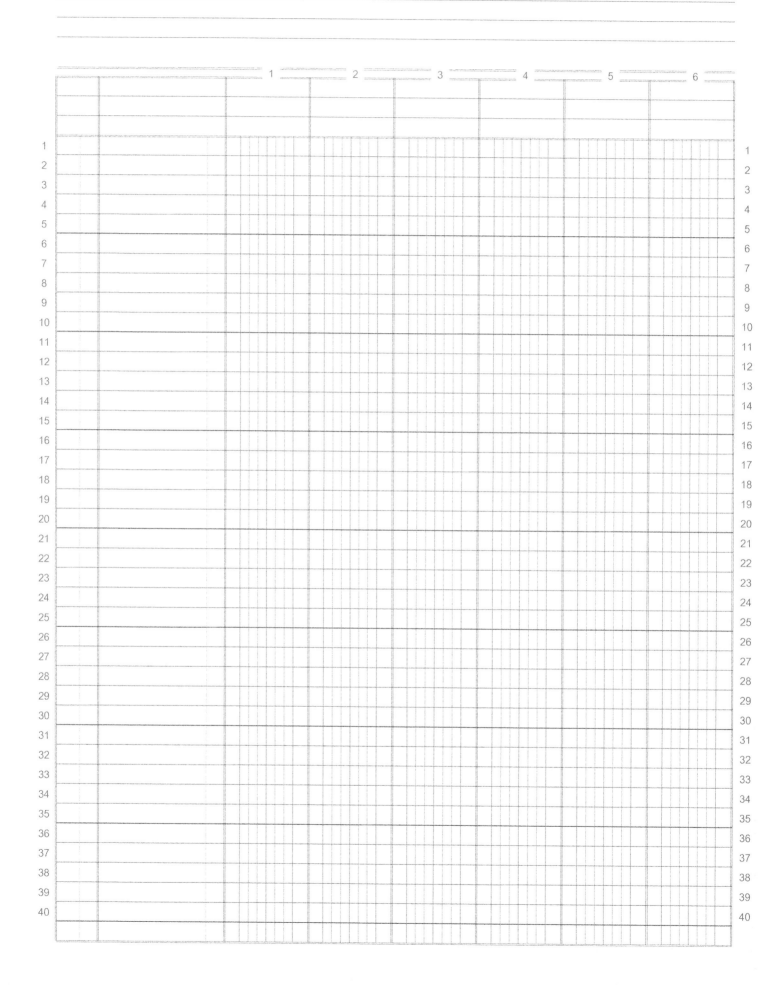

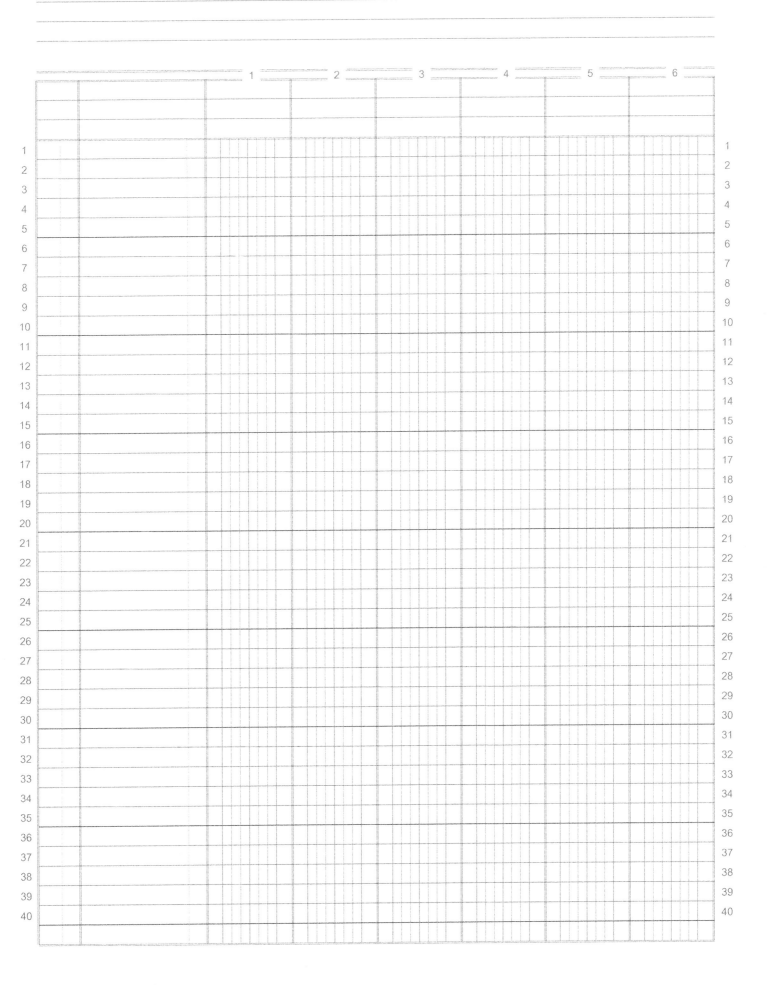

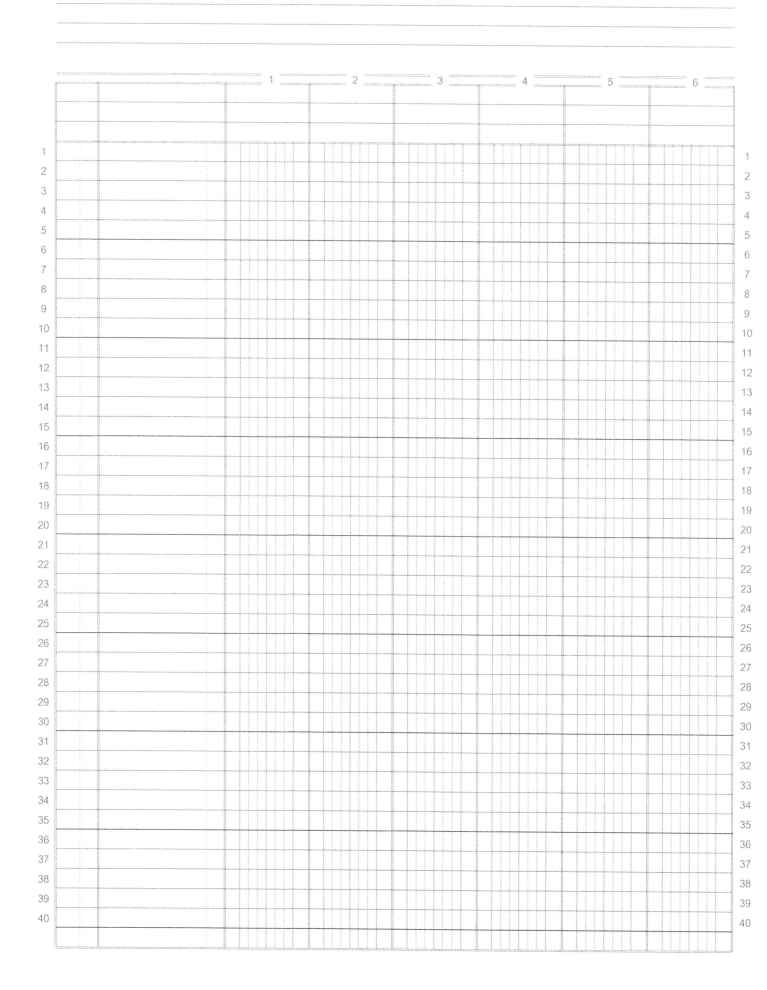

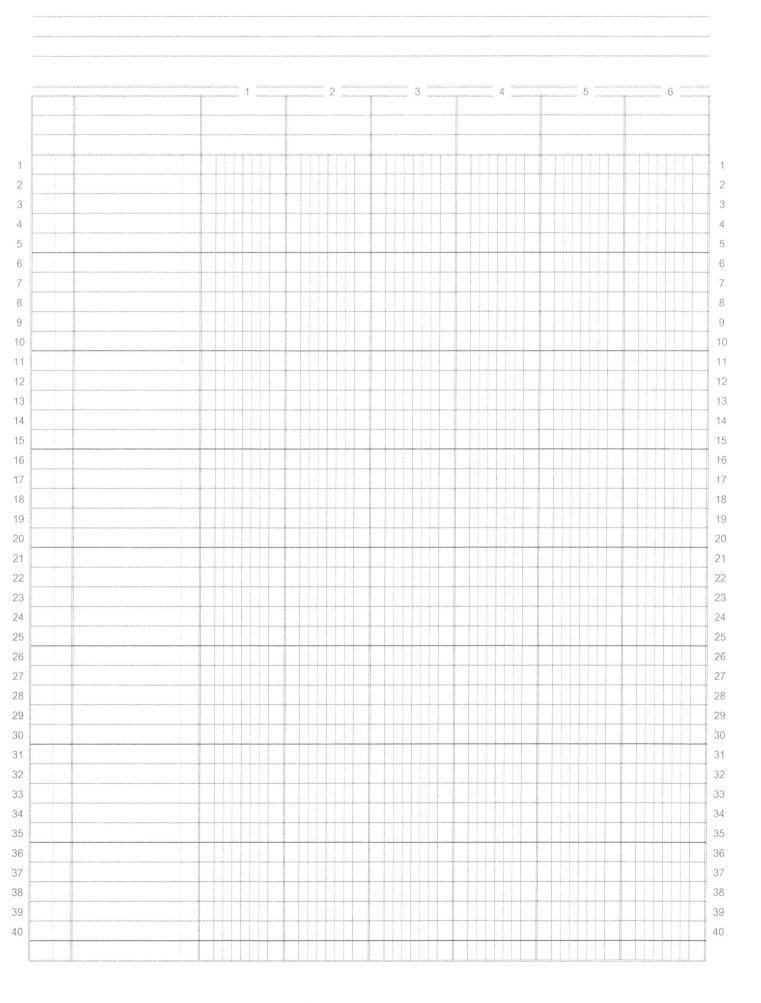

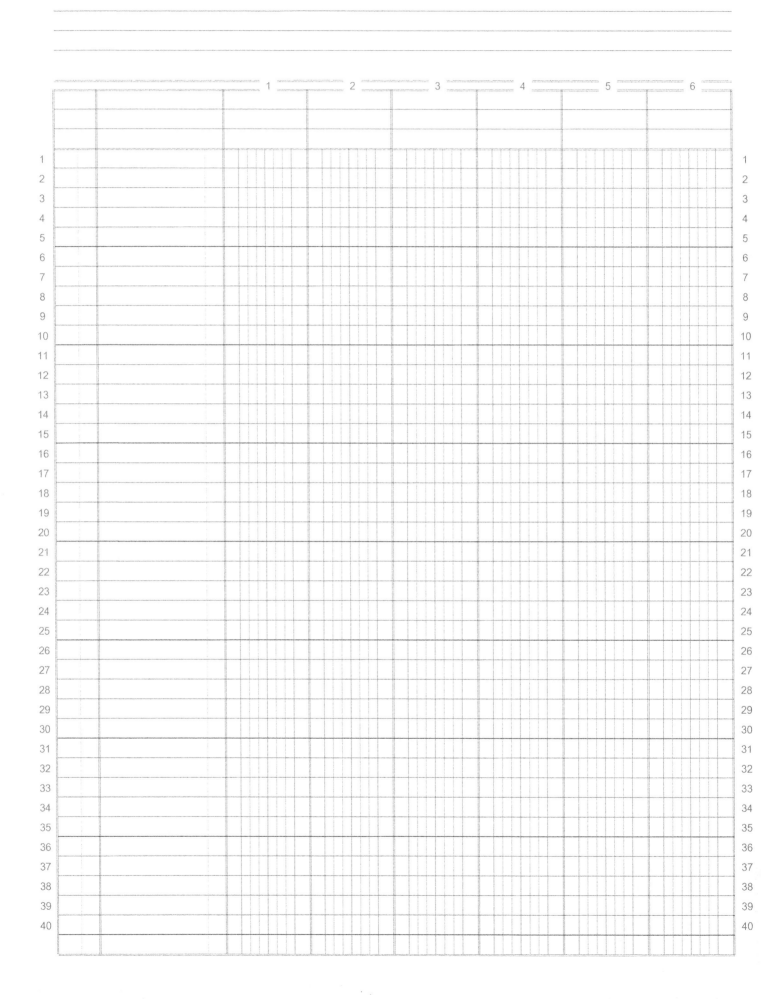

Made in the USA
Las Vegas, NV
02 April 2021

THE HISTORY OF
IKEBANA

Kudo Masanobu

Shufunotomo Co., Ltd.

Translated by Jay and Sumi Gluck

First printing, 1986
Third printing, 1989

Published by Shufunotomo Co., Ltd.
2-9, Kanda Surugadai, Chiyoda-ku, Tokyo 101 Japan

ISBN: 4-07-975090-0
Printed in Japan

CONTENTS

Preface ⋯⋯⋯⋯⋯⋯⋯⋯⋯⋯⋯⋯⋯⋯⋯⋯⋯⋯⋯ 5

Introduction ⋯⋯⋯⋯⋯⋯⋯⋯⋯⋯⋯⋯⋯⋯⋯⋯ 6

Japan Nature ⋯⋯⋯⋯⋯⋯⋯⋯⋯⋯⋯⋯⋯⋯⋯⋯ 8

Where Deity Decends to Earth, Flowers are Offered ⋯⋯⋯⋯ 10

Birth of Ikebana ⋯⋯⋯⋯⋯⋯⋯⋯⋯⋯⋯⋯⋯ 12

Flowers that Decorate the Zashiki Drawing Room ⋯⋯⋯⋯ 14

From Tatebana to Rikka ⋯⋯⋯⋯⋯⋯⋯⋯⋯⋯⋯ 16

Evolution of Rikka Arrangement ⋯⋯⋯⋯⋯⋯⋯⋯⋯ 18

Flowers for Tea Ceremony and Nageire-Hana ⋯⋯⋯⋯⋯⋯ 22

Formation of Seika (Shoka) and Establishment of Ikebana Styles ⋯ 24

Western European Culture and Modern Ikebana ⋯⋯⋯⋯⋯ 30

Ikebana Today ⋯⋯⋯⋯⋯⋯⋯⋯⋯⋯⋯⋯⋯⋯⋯ 33

How to Use Flower Holders ⋯⋯⋯⋯⋯⋯⋯⋯⋯⋯ 48

Flower Holders and Stays ⋯⋯⋯⋯⋯⋯⋯⋯⋯⋯⋯ 51

Technique of Training Branches ⋯⋯⋯⋯⋯⋯⋯⋯⋯ 54

Various Containers ⋯⋯⋯⋯⋯⋯⋯⋯⋯⋯⋯⋯⋯ 56

Chronological Table of History of Ikebana ⋯⋯⋯⋯⋯⋯⋯ 60

Index ⋯⋯⋯⋯⋯⋯⋯⋯⋯⋯⋯⋯⋯⋯⋯⋯⋯⋯ 63

PREFACE

New developments in studies of the history of ikebana during these last thirty-odd years have been outstanding. There have been more thorough investigations of pre-16th century Muromachi, or early period before ikebana was given set rules for arrangement and formulated as an art, which is by universal definition, specific discipline. At present there are numerous new researches under way into ikebana prehistory which, instead of dealing only with the relationships of offertory flowers and evolution of ikebana into art, reach back into that universal animism in primitive beliefs. There is reliance upon folkloric material to shed light on origins of ikebana. For this, we look at what is at the basis of the culture of Japan, special characteristics of the climate of the islands as part of a broader new Stone Age cultural sphere. Attention is given to interrelationships of man and plants hidden in the primitive beliefs that existed in this common multinational culture. But here, mystery seems rather to deepen as to why only in Japan this aspect of universal basic animism evolved into this sophisticated national art.

It is then natural that comparison with situations in Western Europe and China should follow, and this will probably encourage further studies on an international scale. In the international sphere, just how much influence Chinese flower arrangement had upon development of *tatebana* in Muromachi times is a major topic of study. Research on the not-too-clear history of ikebana during the Middle Ages is still continuing. Here, overall history of theatrical arts as well as social history of Kyoto, center of these arts in the Middle Ages, should also eventually be clarified by these investigations.

The period for which quite reliable reference material exists to bring out clearly what was taking place, is the following early Edo era. Among historians who have worked on this time and made enormous contributions are Shigemori Mirei, Yamane Yuzo, and Ohi Minobu.

This short historical sketch of ikebana, covering roughly 600 years since its inception until the present day, is illustrated to show various highlights for each period and designed so that evolution of ikebana styles can be clearly followed pictorially.

This is not meant to cover every aspect of the history of ikebana, but it starts with background information leading to its formulation and shows how ikebana as a living art of the Japanese was accepted and supported by the people. This publication was made with the desire that through it, those many people from foreign countries who love ikebana can come to understand it better.

INTRODUCTION

If the simple act of putting flowers in a container is *ikebana*, then this exists not only in Japan, but may be found from ancient times in any tribe and in any country throughout the world. But ikebana as living, disciplined art has long flourished in Japan, and in recent years has received notable recognition internationally. Before ikebana became solely a function of room decoration, Japanese in offering plants accepted their mutual coexistence feeling that the whole arrangement continued to be a living thing which brought together nature and man in some greater unity.

This feeling towards plants is brought about by the climate of Japan, where every season is filled with changes of evergreen and deciduous trees and flowering plants intermixed. This feeling for plants that represents what in Japanese is called *yorishiro*, sacred place, as found in all primitive beliefs, gradually intermingled and amalgamated with sophisticated Buddhism crossing over from China in the 6th and following centuries, with its solemnity and its formal offertory flowers. In 14th century, summertime flower festivals were held in noble residences and limitations to arrangements began to emerge as formulating discipline. By 16th century Muromachi era, Japanese came to build *zashiki* drawing rooms into their residential architecture. Here *tatebana*, ikebana's first set form, was created for certain memorial days when rituals were felt necessary. Arrangements came to be designated as to their form, materials combined, and method of expression.

In contrast to these tatebana arrangements for special occasions, those for everyday use now came to be called *nageire*, or casually tossed-in flowers. In 15th century Azuchi-Momoyama era, as so many national arts evolved into their present-day forms and *cha-do* tea offering became formalized into what we might term ceremony, nageire lived on as *chabana*.

From late Azuchi-Momoyama through early Edo period, the religious significance of tatebana gradually diminished to develop into *rikka*, an independent artistic creation meant to be admired by others like any decorative lay art. Emperor Gomizuno-o started holding exhibitions of rikka as well as *hana-awase*, poetry and flower "comparisons," open competitions. Ikenobo master Senko II directed these poetry and flower shows. From the beginning of Edo (1600) into Genroku years (1688–1704) rikka, and for a while chabana which continued to be the tea ceremony nageire-type arrangement, separated from tea art to become popular as decorative flowers for small drawing rooms in the new *sukiya*-style domestic architecture. In the past, rikka had been for emperor, court nobles and warrior class, as well as for the priestly class, but a new class of wealthy merchants now became its patrons, vastly increasing its followers so that it became one of the representative arts of gregarious, gorgeous Genroku culture.

By middle Edo, mid-18th century, through development in botanical studies and gardening, Japanese changed from their earlier ways and started to look at things more rationally. Examining the raising of plants, empirical knowledge as gained from observation came to be highly valued. Then looking further to see what lay behind this aspect of nature, came recognition of other aspects of nature, resulting in incorporating the philosophy of naturalism prevailing at that time. A new world-view came into being with the concept of those three elements of heaven, earth and man being extracted from it to establish the philosophy of floral style for ikebana as an art form. On the other hand, among those who did not adhere to the rules of nageire style was a group influenced by flower arrangement books from China, who placed great value upon the meaning that flowers transmitted to create a new genre known as literati arrangement.

In Emperor Meiji's reign, westernization or modernization of Japan started and ikebana met the culture of the West. At about the same time that ikebana was introduced to the West directly, it received great influence from it and underwent great change as *moribana*, a new style of arrangement encompassing international expression appeared.

Surviving that dark age of the unfortunate Second World War, ikebana is now released from the shackles of narrowly interpreted tradition. While receiving much influence from contemporary Western art, experiments have been made to build up a compatible form. Avant-garde ikebana is one of these experiments and for the advancement of ikebana as art, has been quite stimulating.

From late 1960s until the present, modern ikebana has been based on the foundation built by avant-garde movement. At the same time it has kept asking itself what ikebana is. Ikebana, which relies upon nature and nature's recreation by an arranger, now takes in ecological considerations.

We are searching for a new venue for ikebana.

Japan Nature

Momiji Hill Seen from Kagetsu Room of Gepparo Villa of Katsura Rikyu Katsura Rikyu (Katsura Imperial Villa) was built for Prince Toshihito, who created the house of Hachijo, on the middle reaches of the Katsura River early in the Edo period. For fifty years, beginning ca. 1615, construction and improvement works were carried on in three stages. The third stage was started on the occasion of the visit of retired Emperor Gomizuno-o. Around a big pond in the garden stand four villas, including Gepparo Villa. Katsura Rikyu, where architectural beauty and natural beauty are in perfect harmony, is world famous.

Ikebana, as an art which is part of everyday life, can be said to have originated in the singular ecology of Japan where primeval natural scenery differed greatly from that of Western Europe, in consisting of "laurilignosa forests." These are shiny broad-leafed trees, such as evergreen oak or beech and laurel, or camellia, chestnut, osmanthus and tea, all evergreens with branches profusely covered in thick, glossy, broad leaves. These trees are found as dense woods and developed centering around the never freezing subtropical south China and highland southeast Asia to Nepal over 10,000 years ago, spreading to the southern tip of Korea, to the southwestern part of the Japanese archipelago by 7,000 years ago, then gradually working up the main island. It is the source for the name for a specific Stone Age period,

the Laurilignosa Culture or "Culture of shiny broadleaf trees" characterized by specific proto-agriculture which led to developing wet rice or paddy. In Japan since Jomon-early neolithic times this has been an area of human habitation which gave birth to various indigenous cultural traits, some of which are shared internationally, with others later showing national differentiation.

Original indigenous plants that have been growing intermixed are these subtropical shiny broad-leafed evergreens, while adding a local Japan touch are temperate clime conifers including those with needle-like leaves such as pine, as well as varieties of deciduous trees like maples whose leaves turn beautiful colors in the chill of autumn. Taking a general view from southwestern

Upper Villa of Shugakuin Rikyu in Spring
Shugakuin Rikyu (Shugakuin Imperial Villa) was originally built as a retreat for ex-Emperor Gomizuno-o at Shugakuin, Kyoto, after his abdication in 1629. The superbly landscaped spacious garden, in which stand Upper, Middle, and Lower Villas, has ponds and several groves. From the Upper Villa a full view of the city of Kyoto spreads out below, with the hills of Kurama and Kibune in the background.

through northeastern Japan, following the route of the steadily advancing laurilignosa clime, in any one area from sea level up through higher ground first come broad leaf evergreens, with deciduous trees following. Further north, deciduous trees are preceded by an intermediary level of conifers. It is this natural setting of intermingling laurilignosa-temperate vegetation that formed what became the foundation of the culture of Japan.

In early spring budding of deciduous trees and the flowering of plants follow in rapid succession, while from late spring through early summer beautiful fresh green leaves emerge and in field and mountain a rich variety of flowers take turns blossoming. In the heat of summer by those lakes and marshes, ponds and streams which make basic wet rice-culture possible, there are flowers that bloom to give a cooling atmosphere. In autumn, deciduous trees turn color beautifully, while trees that had bloomed earlier now bear fruits which also turn beautiful colors. Then trees with branches bare, having lost their leaves, stand with conifers whose branches are always green to make an arrangement that appears like giant flowers amidst winter landscape.

These delicate changes nature weaves through the seasons may be the source of the peculiarly Japanese sensitivity for and appreciation of plants. This eventually, brought forth ikebana, a living art form for daily life, developing out of the tiny bud that is the naive native faith in trees and plants.

Where Deity Descends to Earth, Flowers are Offered

Choju Giga (Scrolls of Frolicking Animals and Humans) Painted late Heian period (794–1185). In front of a frog enthroned as Buddha with halo of Japanese banana leaves, lotus flowers are offered. A monkey in guise of a Buddhist priest is conducting a religious service.

Gilt-Bronze Lotus and Flower Vase Made ca. 1330. Lotus flowers are arranged in the vase, and to hold them in place, stays are also inserted in the mouth of the vase. Property of Kanshinji Temple.

Japanese brought up in this clime so different from the West, holding their own feelings towards plants, came to cherish the idea of *yorishiro*. This simple belief, basic to all stone age peoples, holds that deity exists on earth, or links to earth, usually in mountain, large boulder, waterfall or tree, especially in evergreens: and in this laurilignosa cultural area, particularly in glossy broad-leafed trees. Even with deciduous trees, when leaves fall it is felt that spirit is only asleep, that when spring comes it reawakens.

In Japan even today we find *kadomatsu* New Year pine decoration at front gate and use of *tamagushi* branch of sacred green tree as offering to shrine, both with origins in yorishiro. Even though it be in an ordinary place, in erecting yorishiro they believed that deity would descend through it. This is different from tree worship in Europe, where such as the Christmas tree is but sacred symbol. Both originate in similar stone age concepts, but why do they diverge so? This attitude of Japanese

toward tree worship was a seminal influence upon the birth of ikebana.*

Offering flowers has been almost universal among mankind at least since Neanderthal developed burial rites. Formal usage was introduced from China to Japan in the sixth century along with Buddhism, as floral altar decor before images of Buddha. Lotus flowers had always been preferred for this, probably because in India where Buddhism originated, lotus had been age-old symbol of rebirth and eternity since dawn of consciousness in Egypt. In Japan, also, lotus blossoms were used as offertory flowers. But already earliest Buddhist paintings show this not limited to lotus, that other beautiful flowers blooming during other seasons were included. Just as flowers were used as Buddhist offerings, there are numerous examples in genre paintings of their being used at yorishiro sacred sites as ritual offering along with food and wine. Flowers and trees that symbolize various festivities may be either offertory flowers or

10

(left)
Kadomatsu Simple *kadomatsu* (New Year's pine tree decoration). Uprooted pine saplings are tied with ceremonial two-color paper cord, to enshrine *toshigami* (deity of incoming year) during his New Year descent.

(right)
Minakuchi (Water Gate) Festival Before making a rice seedbed or transplanting rice seedlings, flowers are placed at water gates of paddy fields as offering to *ta-no-kami* (deity of paddies). This is to serve as medium for deity's descent into the paddy.

Saegusa Festival At annual festival of Isakawa Shrine, Nara Prefecture, lilies are offered to deity of shrine.

yorishiro itself.

In this way the raising of flowers that were used with some religious significance spread, becoming part of agricultural rites. Surmising from the 8th century *Manyoshu*, oldest anthology of Japanese poetry, plants for medicines and dyeing had also enteed into peoples' daily lives. As they became indispensable to livelihood, so enjoying and appreciating their flowers became part of life.

Arranging flowers, we will see, later developed into its own art form. In Japanese folk religion there ar sects to which "Art is the mother of religion" and thus works of art are each in themselves yorishiro, sacred links. This undercurrent flows throughout popular Japanese thought and reinforces that special feeling ikebana has come to assume.

Another point is that while Japan contributed numerous new species to Occidental gardens, she is relatively flower poor in that blooms are neither raised nor used en masse as in Europe. Except for mountains of cherry trees, flowers appear in Japanese gardens relatively sparsely placed. There are neither cut flowers by dozens for vases as in America, nor the native taste to use them thus. This is an important aspect of ikebana esthetic, born on paucity.

*Friend and editor Jay Gluck suggests two possibilities, neither of which excludes the other. First is that after Stone Age spiritual awakenings, West and East developed differently. Europe evolved towards monotheism, which in its simplistic popular form does not allow of thoughts of other spirit or even that universal sacredness to which yorishiro is living link. East developed toward Buddhism, which is not polytheistic despite its seeming plethora of gods, but truly pantheistic in that our entire universe is seen as deity, as totally sacred. In our temporal aberration apart from that mystic universality, yorishiro are at least reminders, perhaps gateway links, to sacred reality.

He notes it may also have to do with left-brain/right-brain dominance in West and East respectively. European languages and culture are left-brain dominated, thus more logic-directed. Japan, and its Polynesian roots and perhaps southeast Asia, seem right-brain dominated, more emotion-directed. This may have lead as well to Western "logical" cause-effect concepts of creation, as opposed to Japan's more sentimental ideas of origins: thus to monotheism on one hand and overall sacredness on the other.

Birth of Ikebana

Kinkakuji Temple (Gold Pavilion) Built in 1397 by Ashikaga Yoshimitsu, 3rd Muromachi Shogun (1338–1573), numerous ikebana competitions and other cultural events were held here. Yoshimitsu was a lover of learning and the performing arts and initiated the Kitayama cultural era.

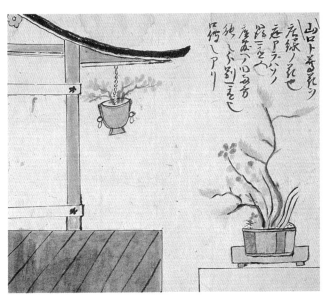

Kaoirai no Kadensho (*Kaoirai* Flower Arrangement Book) Composed in 1499, this is the oldest book on flower arrangement in Japan. Here are pictures of flowers arranged in a hanging vase, and flowers arranged in a rectangular basin, which is said to be the forerunner of *suna-no-mono* (sand-filled basin) and of *moribana* (piled-up flowers) style arrangements. Property of Ikenobo Headquarters.

One of the earliest records of Japanese admiring flowers is found in the *Kokin-waka-shu* poetry anthology compiled early 10th century, where it is written, "In flower pot place cherry blossoms." The early 11th century *Makura-no-soshi* (Pillow Book) contains the phrase "...at the base of the handrailing placing a large green vat..." which reveals to us the color of container, its size and even its positioning.

From about this time at court, events were held called *kiku-awase*, *senzai-awase* and *hana-awase* wherein people came together bringing chrysanthemums, garden trees and plants, and cut flowers, respectively, and divided into two teams. It then became a competition or game as based upon these sets as topics, they wrote poems which were then judged, with honors awarded. Among these, senzai-awase "garden plants and trees"

were to become the basis for bonsai and *bonkei*, which appear later. In the oldest book on ikebana, *Kaoirai no Kandensho*, we find illustrations of flower arrangements in containers with sand, *suna-no-mono*, as well as what could be prototypes of moribana, revealing through their description that they were "...flowers made to be admired," in short, decorative art.

From the latter 14th century, *Shichiseki Horaku-no-hana* exhibition was held in July at temples and shrines as part of the Tanabata Vega-star festival. This soon came to have arrangements displayed in people's living rooms, ostensibly as offering to Buddha, but so set up as to be "viewed and admired." There may have been some that actually were religious offerings, but it became more an occasion also for merrymaking, where viewing of flowers was enjoyed with dining and drinking.

12

Sosei Kadensho (Book of Flower Arrangement by Sosei) Composed in 1529. Mainly a book of *tatebana* style, but *suna-no-mono* style, using pine branches as well as bamboo, is also seen. Property of Yamato Bunkakan.

Mon'ami Kadensho (Book of Flower Arramgement by Mon'ami) Composed in 1553. Book on the *tatebana* style of flower arrangement. In front of a triad of hanging scrolls are three utensils and vases to the side. With Buddhist figure scroll in center, scrolls on left and right are a pair. Flowers arranged on left and right sides are also paired. Property of the Kaoin Temple.

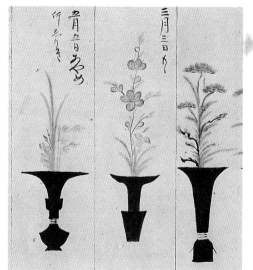

From *Hanafu*, Drawn by Sen'ami Written in 1552. Flowers arranged in *tatebana* (upright flowers) style for Girls' Festival on March 3 (center) and Boys' Festival on May 5 (left). Property of Ronobo Taiten.

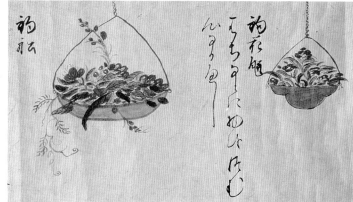

Sosei Kadensho (Book of Flower Arrangement by Sosei) Written in 1529. Shows *nageire* (throw or toss in) style, in which flowers are casually "tossed" into a hanging boat-shaped vase. Property of Yamato Bunkakan.

By this time *hana-awase* (flower competition) had become part of *uta-awase* (poetry competition). Containers of flowers were now displayed simply for admiring and there came about a pronounced change in the character of these meetings with *mono-awase*, (object competition), for most unusual flowers and most admired containers becoming the objective of these meetings.

Among courtiers, samurai and priests competing for top recognition at these hana-awase, new trends to stress exotic or rare flowers and unusual containers got stronger, with rare vases from China appearing frequently. It is said that Shogun Ashikaga Yoshimitsu of the Muromachi period offered a huge award to the winner at one of the competitions at the Kinkakuji Gold Pavilion, which at that time was his royal villa.

We are acquainted with the lives of these court nobles and priests through contemporary scroll paintings. We see beginning to appear here earliest hints of formal flower arrangement: *tatebana* (standing flower). Among written records, we find in *Kanmon-gyoki*, diary of Prince Fushimi-no-miya Sadafusa Shinno, details of life at court, 1418–1448, as well as descriptions of art forms which we can see in retrospect to be the beginnings of ikebana and *sa-do* (tea-way-art) or "tea ceremony."

According to this, flowers arranged in vases came to be displayed in the zashiki drawing room. Flowers that previously had been viewed from outside the handrail of the building, are now seen to be slowly moving inside to be viewed within interior space.

Flowers that Decorate the Zashiki Drawing Room

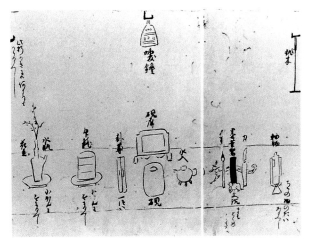

Kundaikan Sochoki (Interior Decoration for Shogun Residences) Placement of decorative articles and utensils is illustrated.

Kasuga Gongen Reigenki Emaki (Picture Scrolls Depicting Miracles Performed by Deity Kasuga Gongen) Drawn in the 14th century. On the wooden floor in the right corner stands a vase holding a branch of scarlet-tinged maples. Property of the Imperial Household Agency.

Shuhan Ron (Discourse on Sake and Rice) Drawn about mid-16th century. This picture scroll depicts samurai discussing the merits of sake and rice. Scene of *oshi-ita*, or the original form of *tokonoma* alcove, with a pair of scrolls hanging, and in front of these a pair of vases in *tatebana* style. The *shin* (principal stem) is a young pine branch. Property of Sanji Chionji Temples.

Popularity of hana-awase brought about a great influx of fine receptacles crossing the seas from China. Along with the arrival of these containers came about the establishment of *shoin-zukuri* residential style of architecture as living quarters for court nobles. It has *zashiki* drawing room, and at this time *tatami* (straw mats) first come into use as floor covering. The special character of this zashiki was that it had an alcove area, a study nook and display shelves: three spatial elements which are to become special areas for interior decoration.

Oshi-ita was the origin of the *tokonoma*. On the wall was a space where a Buddhist picture was hung, in front of which this board was laid on the floor on which an incense burner and offertory flowers were placed. This eventually came to be combined with *shoin* (study nook) and *kazari-dana* (display shelves), and its location was designated on the north wall of the zashiki. Shoin had a low desk, supplies for writing, and being a space for reading lighting had to be devised so translucent-papered *shoji* window was constructed to admit softly filtered

Vol. 8 of *Boki-Ekotoba* Drawn about mid-14th century. Before a wooden door there is a desk, on which stand three utensils including a celadon vase holding plum (*ume*) branches arranged in *tatebana*. Property of Nishi Honganji Temple.

Vol. 5 of *Boki-Ekotoba* Scene of a poetry party. On the wall hangs a trio of picture scrolls, with an incense burner in front, and on both sides a pair of flower vases. Property of Nishi Honganji Temple.

light. Display shelves were for placing various objects of art, thus this shoin-zukuri came to be study and parlor in one.

Alcove became setting for vase with standing flowers, while in study nook were reading and writing materials, and on the shelves decorative articles were placed. Soon there was realization of the need for systematized placement, and specialists, who might be called interior decorators, appeared. Among these were Noami and Soami, who became close associates of the shogun as all-around practioners and producers of the arts. Such people came to be known as *doboshu*, whose work it then became to select paintings for the wall and articles for display, placing imported bronzes and celadon vases in the alcove and on the shelves, and arranging flowers in them. From among these doboshu, appear two men, Ryuami and Mon'ami, who became recognized for their outstanding skill with the art of arranging tatebana. It was because of these men that tatebana gradually took on specialized form as decoration for the zashiki.

From Tatebana to Rikka

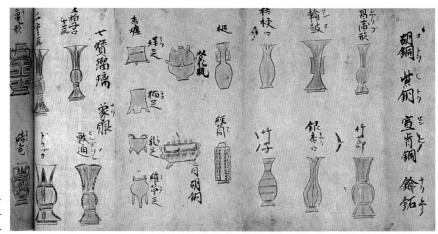

Ikenobo Senjun Kadensho (Book of Flower Arrangement by Ikenobo Senjun) Illustrated are various kinds of imported flower vases.

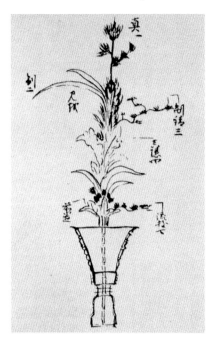

(left)
Sen'ei Densho (Book of Flower Arrangement by Sen'ei) Written in the Tenmon period (1532–1555). Drawings illustrate development of *tatebana* into *rikka*. Property of Ikenobo Headquarters.

Book of Flower Arrangement, Hand Copy by Junsei in 1554 Forms of *suna-no-mono* style are shown. Property of Yomei Bunko.

Sendensho (1445–1536) is a manual on tatebana, but mixed in and thus handed down to us is the nageire form of flower arrangement. Tatebana was originally arranged for special events, you might say for ceremonial occasions, so that its shape, container and even the materials combined all had to follow prescribed rules. On some occasions, in the alcove were placed a set of three hanging scrolls, in front of which was set a folding stand and upon this were placed three essential articles of incense burner, candle stand and vase. In the vase, was first placed the main stem called *shin-no-hana* made to stand upright, and then two flowers or leaves were placed at its base spreading outwards, one to lower left of the main flower and the other to its right.

This form of main stem and two shorter ones was given movement by this trinitarian arrangement of main stems, and reflects its Buddhist offertory origin in being described as representing the birth of the historical person of the Buddha, Shaka, or Sakyamuni as fulfillment of the sacred trinity. The influence of this form will be greatly felt in ikebana later. Even today it is retained, referred to as *hongatte-no-hana* or as "arrangement oriented left."

Compared to tatebana with its main stem, nageire is arranged freely without prescribed form or container. It is explained that if tatebana were considered a form that is not for daily use, then nageire is one specifically for everyday use. Thus its container need not be a regular one, but anything informal whether boat-shaped, basket, or any of many casual wares.

In the mid-16th century there were many flower masters, but among them Ikenobo Senno was exceptional.

Rikka by **Senko II** Copy made in 1634. Arrangements made by Ikenobo headmaster Senko, the Second. Property of Ikenobo Headquarters.

Folding Screen with Pictures of *Rikka* Style Painted about mid-17th century. These are panels 3 and 4 of twelve panels on pair of six-fold screens. Property of Nomura Art Gallery.

He published his *Senno Kuden* or "oral tradition by Senno." In explaining his philosophy on ikebana in this work, he says that it is important to arrange so as to reveal the basic nature of the plant or tree. He clearly defines how his tatebana differs from others existing at that time and begins to establish regulations for it.

Senno was succeeded by Ikenobo Senei, who goes still one step further to divide tatebana with *shin* into three styles: *shin, gyo* and *so*.

With formal shin style the shape of container is specified, as is height of main stem, set in proportion to that of its vase.

Gyo arrangement is less formal and it is used often at both sides of the three articles placed upon the alcove board, or in front of the set of hanging scrolls in a large tokonoma. In this arrangement, shin stem does not rise straight up, but imitates the natural stance of whatever material used.

So has been designated as a small arrangement that can be placed on display shelves in the shoin, or as one in a hanging container. According to drawings of floral forms by Sen'ei, there is one with as many as seven principal stems. From this we can gather that he was already working on a development of rikka. That he was experimenting with new types of expression can be seen in his drawings of what would become rikka arrangement using dried branches and dessicated trunks as main stem, and for *so* arrangements in his illustrations of suna-no-mono arrangement in sand.

Evolution of Rikka Arrangement

Portrait of Emperor Gomizuno-o Patron of ikebana, often holding large ikebana exhibition at the Imperial Court. Property of Sennyuji Temple.

Suna-no-mono by Senko II Irises are arranged in a sand-filled basin by Ikenobo headmaster Senko II. Property of Ikenobo Headquarters.

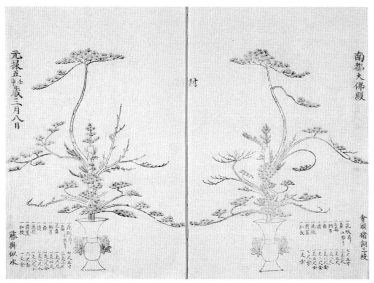

Newly Selected 50 Arrangements in Vases Drawn in 1692. Pine is used with curving main stem. The right and left arrangements in *rikka* style form a pair: right, arranged by Igai Sanshi, left by Fujikake Jisui. Property of Ikenobo Head-quarters.

The Azuchi-Momoyama period (1573–1600) saw native arts and culture reach full maturity. Castle architecture introduced from Europe flourished, and residences of court nobles were becoming larger. In this kind of enlarged living area, tatebana gradually took on bigger even grander form, evolving into rikka.

At the end of the sixteenth century, when generalissimo Toyotomi Hideyoshi visited the residences of such cultured lords as Mohri and Maeda, he saw what Ikenobo Senko, first headmaster of the Ikenobo School, had arranged in their oshi-ita alcoves. According to

records, in an alcove measuring 7.3 m (24 ft) wide was hanging a set of four scroll paintings of monkeys, and in front of that was a huge flat receptacle measuring two meters long and one meter front to back in which was arranged a rikka-suna-no-mono arrangement. One huge pine branch was used as main stem, which instead of rising up straight was used naturally, extending horizontally to either side. Twenty monkeys painted in the hanging scrolls were said to have appeared as though seated on its branches.

First headmaster Senko on occasion of a ceremony

Suna-no-mono **by Daijuin Ishin** Drawn in 1678. Daijuin Ishin chose only pine, using two branches, commemorating the 200th anniversary of the foundation of Honnoji Temple. Property of Saito Socho.

Rikka Jisei Sho Written in 1688. A book of *rikka* arrangements by Kuwahara Fushunken Senkei. Here cockscombs are used for principal stem.

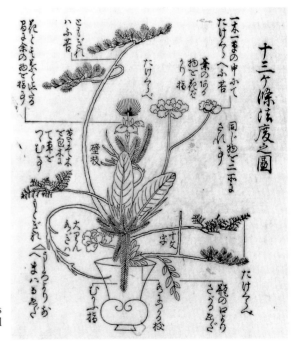

Prohibitions Listed in *Rikka Jisei Sho* Thirteen prohibitions in arranging flowers in *rikka* style are illustrated. These are still observed.

marking completion of Daiunin temple, held an exhibition and displayed 100 arrangements. Of these 100 exhibitors, 88 were of the priesthood.

In the first half of the 17th century, Senko II took over as headmaster and became active. Under patronage of Emperor Gomizuno-o he started propagating rikka, centering his attention on court nobles. Gomizuno-o was extremely fond of rikka and sponsored floral exhibitions at court frequently. Most of these were under direction of Senko II, and established an unprecedented reputation for him. Even after abdication Emperor Gomi-

zuno-o continued, by creating his Gomizuno-o Institute at Sentoh Imperial Palace, Kyoto. Here on one hand he held forth in indirect rule as cloistered emperor, while on the other hand he invited scholars, poets of *renga* (linked verse) and other savants to join him at this salon centered on the culture of the court nobles of that time.

Senko II became instructor of rikka to those samurai and specially selected priests who had been granted the special rank of *dojo*, equivalent to that of court nobles and who could thus enter the imperial palace at will. In this way rikka spread even more. Rikka works of Senko

Exterior View of Shishinden (Ceremonial Hall) **of Kyoto Gosho** (Kyoto Imperial Palace) Kyoto Gosho had been the abode of successive emperors, from the period of Northern and Southern Dynasties (1336–1392) until end of the Edo period (1876). Shishinden, built in Heian period (794–1185) palace architectural style, is where state ceremonies were held. Ancient panelled hanging doors and balustrades are seen. Before the south front stand the famous *sakon* cherry and *ukon* citrus tree.

Picture Scroll Depicting Various Accomplishments Painted in late 17th century. Accomplishments, both literary and military, which samurai should acquire, are described in this scroll. Illustrated are people learning flower arrangement. Property of Museum of Oriental Arts, Cologne.

II were recorded by artists, so that numerous of his works can be seen today.

The outstanding characteristic of rikka of Senko II is the height of *shin* (main stem). Although height of main stem of tatebana had been set to be equal to up to one and a half times that of the container, the classical occidental "golden section" wherein the proportion of larger to smaller is the same as that of total length to larger, Senko II's rikka were two or three times that and in some illustrations are seen to be even taller.

Also, the taller the central shin stem became, the more

evident became the spread and movement of the lower branches opening to right and left at the rim of the container. Onto the vertical line rising upward, a number of *dogu* or what might be called "accents" were added and the form of rikka as we know it was now taking shape.

However, looking at these combinations of materials of Senko II, he is seen to have faithfully followed what Ikenobo Senoh had earlier outlined regarding fidelity to beauty of natural scenery. Moreover, in large-scale arrangements he made exceptional use of space, sculpturally adjusting and composing it, in which materials

Bathhouse Girl with Flowers Arranged in *Rikka* Style Ca. Kanbun period (1661–1673). Property of Ikeda Masahiro.

Takao, Bathhouse Beauty Drawn about Genroku period (1668–1704). Flowering crab apple is arranged with charcoal used as holders. Property of Oda Eiichi.

from nature appear to be truly alive. In this way, with the appearance of such an exceptional artist as Senko II, tatebana evolved onward from being purely parlor interior decoration to take on its own merit, worthy of praise as an independent work of art.

At the time of Senko II his supporters were court nobles, samurai and priests, but in the latter half of the 17th century wealthy merchants of Kyoto and Osaka and their sons became patrons of rikka. This diffusion of rikka brought about a profusion of printed matter concerning it, and this in turn encouraged its

further popularization.

Outstanding followers of Senko II were active, and numerous talented and renowned masters of rikka appeared, such as: Daijuin Ishin, Ikai Sanzaemon, Juichiya Taemon, Takada Anryubo Shugyoku, Kuwahara Fushunken Senkei. With numerous such masters appearing on the scene, rikka attained a period of magnificence supported by the tastes of the newly-risen merchants of great wealth. By the end of the 17th century, rikka had reached its acme.

Flowers for Tea Ceremony and Nageire-Hana

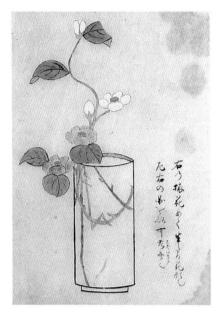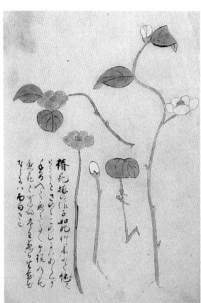

Notes for Instructions in *Nageire* Style of Flower Arrangement Written in 1696. Instructions show how to trim camellia branches and put them in a vase. Property of Hosokawa Morisada.

Notes for Instructions in *Nageire* Style of Flower Arrangement Plum blossoms (*ume*) and camellia flowers arranged in *nageire* style. Property of Hosokawa Morisada.

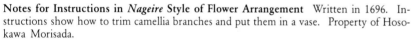

Tatebana, if we must compare, as an arrangement for the drawing room (as has been mentioned previously) was not for daily use, while *nageire-hana* (throw- or toss-in flower) was more suited for daily use.

This nageire-hana originated during Azuchi Momoyama period (1573–1600) as an ikebana form known as *chanoyu-no-hana*, literally "tea-hot water flower" or *chabana*, "tea flower," when Sen-no-Rikyu developed his *wabi*-naturalistic style art of tea service, a ritual of communion with art clumsily translated into English as "tea ceremony" and to this day the soul of Japanese aesthetics. Nageire-hana for tea ceremony developed through small arrangements which need not conform to any special style beyond placing emphasis on the intrinsic beauty of one single flower. About this period the term nageire-hana originates for this style which tries to retain original form and essence of the flower by casually tossing a flower with its stem and leaves into a vase to create a naturalistic curving composition. In contrast, during this same era noble residences became much larger and in this expanded architectural space tatebana took on grander form and rules of arrangement for it were imposed.

Tatebana thus evolved into rikka, popular with courtiers, samurai and priests and by end of the 17th century

Flowers arranged for tea ceremony party at *setsubun* or day before calendrical beginning of spring. (Matsuo-ryu School)

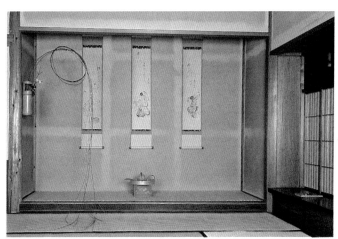

Alcove Decorated for First Tea Ceremony of the Year (Mushanokoji Senke School) Ceremonial stand with *noshi* (sacred paper) is placed in front of a trio of hanging scrolls. Willow branches tied into large knot are in vase with plum (*ume*) blossoms, narcissus and red and white camellias.

---

it reached the wealthy merchant class. This Genroku period (1688–1704) saw urban dominance of such other contemporary popular arts as kabuki and ukiyo-e genre wood-block prints. This was the same time that chanoyu, tea art, also overcame social barriers to become popular among wealthy merchants and chabana and nageire evolved from it to be so much in demand as part of the daily lives of this class.

Chabana and nageire arrangements, unlike rikka, were small and did not require difficult techniques. Added to this was the appearance of a new style of domestic architecture, *sukiya*, which incorporated the sophisticatedly simple aesthetic of Rikyu-style tearoom. Here, zashiki rooms became smaller, and nageire arrangement was more suited to the alcove of this smaller room.

However, criticism soon arose that if chabana or nageire were to decorate these rooms, it was essential that they have rules of arrangement, and so attempts to set a form for nageire became stronger. On the other hand, the popularity of tea art provided an opportunity for nageire to be held in higher esteem, and famous rikka masters working around Ikenobo started studying nageire-hana and wrote texts on it.

Formation of Seika (Shoka) and Establishment of Ikebana Styles

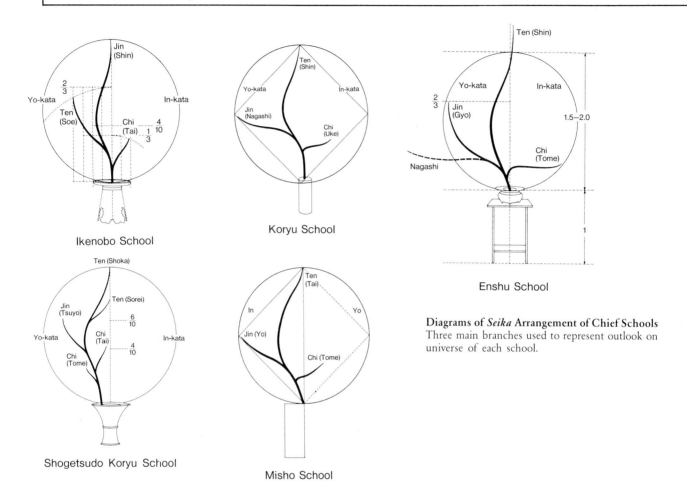

Ikenobo School

Koryu School

Shogetsudo Koryu School

Misho School

Enshu School

Diagrams of *Seika* Arrangement of Chief Schools
Three main branches used to represent outlook on universe of each school.

● **Nageire-hana Styles Begin to be Formulated**

After early Edo Genroku period, Japan's economy made a marked development. Wealthy merchants who had amassed great fortunes appeared in Kyoto, Osaka and Edo and their extravagant style of living was such that it became talk of the town, subject of popular art and literature and, eventually, official attention. Thus during the following Kyoho period (1716–1736), such extravagance induced political reform, and this flourishing social economy stagnated. Now into the luxurious lives of these wealthy merchants intruded strong new anti-sumptuary laws and economic restrictions imposed by the Edo shogunate which became oppressive, bringing about a change in life styles. Rikka and nageire-hana which had been patronized by them, felt the side effects and

began to show changes.

Into this situation, from the Ikenobo group a new flower master appeared, Inouye Tomosada, living in Nara. In his book *Tofuku-kadan* written in 1792, he set forth for the once casual nageire-hana a formal floral style having five main stems. At this time chabana and nageire-hana appear to be evolving towards *seika*, and a theory for establishing seika was being worked upon. We see here attempts to elevate nageire-hana to greater formality befitting the newly invented tokonoma alcove.

After a period of about 20 years, while merchants were still having to forego luxurious ways, a flower master of Ikenobo school, one Rakubodo Gyozan, wrote a text. In it he quoted from that very Confucian philosophy revered by the shogunal system, that those five truths

Enjoying Kyogen, Noh Farce About Tenmei period (1718–1789). On the wall in the alcove at stage right as seen from the audience, a trio of scrolls is hanging, in front of which *rikka* style is arranged. Property of Ikeda Masahiro.

Picture Scroll of a Prosperous *Samurai*'s Life About 18th century. Scene of Girls' Festival in samurai's home. In the alcove in the left corner of the room a scroll is hanging, before which what appears to be peach flowers is arranged. Property of Zenpoji Temple.

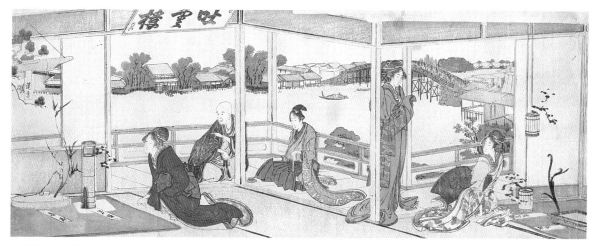

Exhibition of *Seika* Arrangement at Tounro Restaurant Drawn by Katsushika Hokusai, late Kansei period (1789–1801). The picture depicts a flower arrangement exhibition held at Tounro, a restaurant on the Sumida River, Edo. Property of Ikeda Masahiro.

that man must observe should be considered as the ideology for ikebana. Thus the freely arranged nageire-hana is now given forms of *shin*, *gyo* and *so* and these are first illustrated in his arrangements of narcissus.

At this time the state of nageire-hana, against the background of social conditions, was such that it was an arrangement with no set rules for form. Now, like later seika arrangement, it gradually also started being bound by certain rules.

After this, in the late 18th century, when seika arrangement was still in its infancy, stagnant economic conditions began to improve. With stability in Edo, new culture started to take form there under impetus of the merchant class. With this tide, ikebana again regained popularity. At restaurants, ikebana exhibitions

came to be held frequently, attracting attention of the general populace. Articles about its popularity appeared in the newly evolving public press, to the point where a who's who of the ikebana world was published.

●Development of Horticulture

In Japan horticulture had been based on Chinese botanical studies. From the latter half of the 17th century, native horticulture flourished and many books came to be written on this subject. As cities of Kyoto, Osaka and Edo developed, people started to cultivate flowers and trees in their own gardens. Horticulture made technical advances, especially in the line of ornamentals, and by the latter half of the 18th century it was possible to have spotted or variegated leaves on plants and trees. Rooms

Arranging Aspidistra Drawn by Utagawa Hisanobu. Flowers are being arranged for an exhibition in Bunka period (1804–1818). This may be one page of what would have been a triptych. Property of Ikeda Masahiro.

Elegant Flower Arrangement Party Drawn by Eishosai Choki. Woodblock print depicting colorful atmosphere at flower arrangement exhibition in fashion in Tenmei and Kansei periods (1781–1801).

built underground took advantage of subterranean heat, in which chrysanthemums were force-grown to bloom out of season. The public's interest in flowers and trees was stimulated. In such an environment diverse floral materials appeared, and the trend among arrangers at ikebana exhibitions was to vie with each other to have more unusual material.

●The Establishment of Ikebana Schools

Chiba Ryuboku started his own Genji school in the Osaka area. Moving to Edo in 1762, he held ikebana exhibitions repeatedly around then-downtown Asakusa to attract pupils. Creating his own original supplies and equipment, and setting up a system of issuing certificates periodically by grades to pupils, he started what could be

considered the beginnings of the present *iemoto*, or head-master system.

Following Chiba Ryuboku, many flower instructors moved from Kyoto and Osaka to more economically dynamic Edo and went about setting up their own schools of ikebana. Records show clearly that by 1770, Koryu school, had been established by Imai Isshiken-sofu, Enshu school by Shunjuiken Ichiyo, Kodo school by Mochizuki Riunsai as well as others such as Shofu school, Irie school, and Doku school. From this we can see that this was a period when many schools of ikebana were established.

●Seika Style as Theory of the Universe

Nageire-hana was still popular until early in the 19th cen-

Colored Illustration of Flower Arrangement in *Hana Iko* (Flower Kimono Rack) Style *Hana Iko* is a style of flower arrangement using a kimono rack-like stand for arranging flowers. This style serves for showing off *tokonoma*, *chigaidana* shelves and the *shoin* study area. Examples are two *okihana* (placed on shelf), two *kakehana* (suspended on pillar), and one *tsurihana* (hanging). On the shelf is an incense burner. Arranged by Shokeisai Rikyoku, date unknown. Property of Hagiwara Riho.

tury. Now, however gradually, there appeared many schools groping to find new ideas for ikebana and trying to establish new forms.

The founder of Shogetsudo Koryu, belonging to the Buddhist priesthood, took "five great thoughts" as five elements and assigned each of his principal stems to fit one of these elements. Then with his idea of Universe represented as circle, he had these five main stems placed within this circle to become the basic form for his ikebana.

Enshu school started out with two principal stems which represent *ten* (heaven) and *chi* (earth) and then additional stems, totaling odd numbers such as 3, 5, 7 and 9 up to 17 main stems, were added to make up his various floral styles.

Koryu school is based on the concept of three levels of *ten* (heaven), *chi* (earth) and *jin* (man), with these represented by three main branches. Imai Isshinkensofu set up his floral style. With Misho school, that ancient universal philosophical conundrum of squaring the circle was built on as first a circle is delimited within which a square is inscribed touching the circle, which then is divided diagonally into two halves to create two triangles defined by Taoist thought, one being positive, *yang*, the other negative, *yin*. Then standing each triangle either upright or on its side, within their limits three stems of heaven, earth and man are placed, thus composing this distinctive floral style. This triangulation idea evolves out of Chinese aesthetic of landscape painting and was to make its way via international trade through the

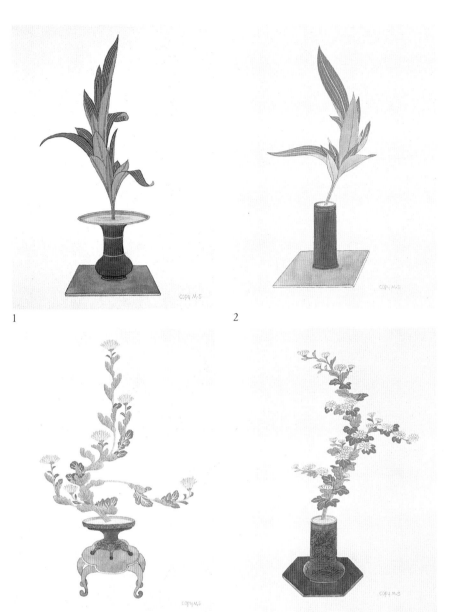

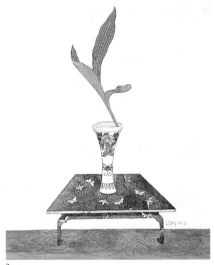

1

2

3

Illustrations of *Seika* Arrangement Color added by Sugiyama Masao of Issuikai, recent.
1. From *Kunshi Yuigi* (1840 by Ikenobo Senmyo.
2. From *Koryu Ikebana Hyaku Heizu* (1803) by Shoseisai Sekimoto Riyu.
3. From *Ikebana Tokiwagusa* (1830) compiled by Mishosai Koho.
4. From *Ikebana Koromo no Ka* (1801) by Teishosai Yoneichiba.
5. Hand copy, origin unknown (ca. 1825).

4

5

Dutch to influence Rembrandt's theory of triangulation in form and light.

Going through these evolutionary steps in this early period, ikebana became established as each different school of ikebana came to have its own philosphy applied as its own floral style. At present the important branches are the three main stems and this is true with trinity fulfilling in all schools the role of heaven, earth and man in the Universe.

This idea owed its origin to the philosphy of applied Confucianism that was in the mainstream of both official and popular thought at this period. And it is organized according to concept of the universe that signifies heaven as respect, earth as obedience with man in harmony.

●Literati Arrangement—*Bunjin-bana*

When ikebana originated there were two kinds of arrangements, which were in the manner of tatebana and nageire. The latter on one hand continued as chabana, while on the other hand it also became independent and developed on its own.

This nageire-hana moved further into two directions: one by being regulated into set forms evolved into seika

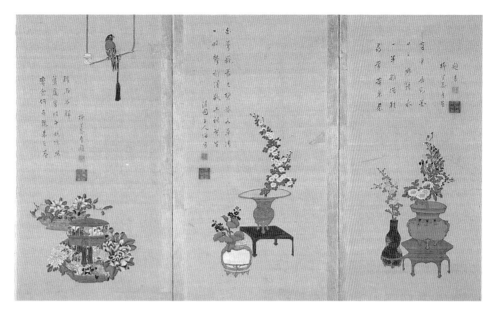

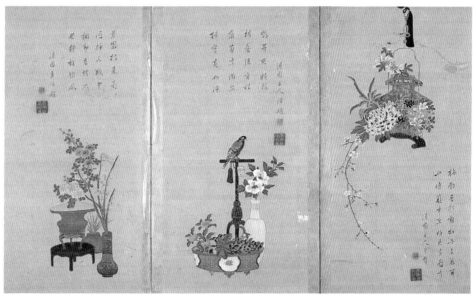

Folding Screen Depicting *Heika* **Arrangement** Drawn by Yanagisawa Kien about mid-18th century. Pair of six-panel folding screens. On each panel is an arrangement with caption in calligraphic verse. Property of Ikeda Masahiro.

and the other, becoming favored by literati of Edo, became what is then called *bunjin-bana* or literati arrangement. Literati is a term applied to those persons who by nature were essentially disposed towards poetry, calligraphy and painting and generally held this mundane existence in disdain, who as intellectuals had elegance as their partner in daily life.

Literati of Japan were closely attached to the poetry and writings of one Chinese savant, Yuán Hung-tao. Greatly admiring his works, they were influenced by his treatise on flowers, *History of Vases*. This work also greatly influenced ikebana in Japan. Introduced early in

the 19th century as literati flowers started to become stylish, he opened to Japanese literati the thoughts of Chinese literati, encouraging their floral style to separate from nageire. Products from China such as unusual containers, flowers, green plants and fruits became admired, as is clearly reflected in paintings of this period. Their aim was to enjoy prose and poetry, paintings and calligraphy, wood and string instruments along with the ritual of sipping *sencha*, fine quality green leaf tea, popular at that time. Literati flowers were enjoyed by many intellectuals and its popularity continued until the 1860s.

Western European Culture and Modern Ikebana

Josiah Conder Introduced ikebana to the West through his book in late 1800s.

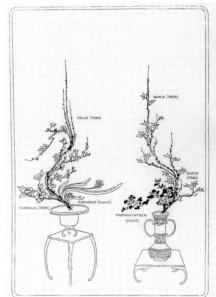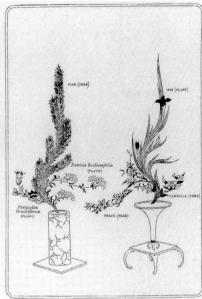

Descriptions of flower arrangement in the *Floral Art of Japan* by Josiah Conder, 1899.

Collapse of the centuries-old system of Shogun and dependent provincial lords greatly shocked the livelihood of residents of Edo. It was only natural that reverberations shook the world of ikebana. In confusion as revolutionary change in government and social system took place, ikebana practitioners were ruined, and with few students the art faced a period of severe decline.

Worthy of note is that even in this period, literati arrangement and seika of Enshu school were able to flourish. On one hand was the one which took a branch as it was and arranged it naturalistically, while the other was an arrangement emphasizing curvatures which took much acquired technique. It is most interesting that arrangements of such opposing extremes were popular at the same time, and especially during a period of revolution.

After the Meiji Restoration many foreigners came to Japan, but what surprised them was the emphasis on curved lines found in seika of Enshu school. Architect Josiah Conder published *Floral Art of Japan*, which first book on ikebana in any European language was responsible for introducing this art widely outside Japan. It may be because of this period that he was here that he stressed seika and Enshu school literati arrangements.

Some ten years after another decline had started to set in, signs of revival of ikebana could again be seen. At the beginning of the 20th century, all schools of ikebana experienced great revival, and even popularity polls on masters of all schools of ikebana were conducted in newspapers.

30

Flower Arrangement by Nishikawa Issotei Bananas casually arranged in old wooden bowl. From the *History of Flower Vases*, 1937.

Tea Party, Various Phases of Women's Life Drawn by Ogata Gekko in 1888, illustrating *sencha* tea party. Property of Kitano Library, Hanamo main office.

At close of the 19th century, *moribana*, a style quite unlike anything that had ever been done before was devised by Ohara Unshin, founder of Ohara school. In the beginning moribana had had the feeling of literati-nageire-like arrangement placed in a flat container, or *suiban*. Actually, it was more bonsai-like an arrangement in that it depicted scenery. However, later, when Western flowers came to be taken up and used as material, this method was deemed most suitable for these new blooms.

With the Meiji Restoration all aspects of Western civilization came into Japan, and numerous varieties of colorful flowers native to Europe and America were imported and came to be cultivated here, as Japanese varieties in turn traveled overseas. Since then, as even today, these former are referred to in Japan as Western flowers.

On the wave of this Westernization, or modernization of Japan, Western flowers that are now part of the daily lives were at first found solely in homes of the propertied class, only gradually reaching the general public. Ways to use these foreign flowers for decoration were introduced, and schools teaching the making of artificial flowers appeared in the capital.

In this situation, Ohara Unshin started to use Western flowers in moribana. But at that time cultivation techniques were not very good, and material was stunted in height. In spite of this, these flowers were prized, and were put to most effective use by arranging in moribana, where they could be used relatively short, with no invisible portion lost to deep vases, and where main accent

Flower Arrangement by Ohara Unshin (Early 1900s) *Moribana* (piled-up flowers) arrangement using ornamental kale as chief material.

Flower Arrangement by Ohara Koun Kaffir lily and carnation arranged *moribana* style.

Free Style Flower Arrangement by Teshigahara Sofu.

Free Style Flower Arrangement by Tsujii Koshu.

Free Style Flower Arrangement by Yamane Suido This work appeared in *Works of Suido*, 1940.

---

was on color.

In this way, modernization started in ikebana. In Taisho era (1912–1926) all kinds of experiments were carried out and ikebana continued evolving. Appearance of free style arrangement, a modern concept, begins from last year of Taisho through early years of Showa (1926-on). Thinking of ikebana not simply as form, but as based on new thought, and trying to formulate this new theory on flower art, were those new driving forces Yamane Suido and Teshigahara Sofu.

Teshigahara Sofu was an ardent admirer of *bunjin-ike*, literati-style arrangement of Kyofu school as headed by Nishikawa Issotei, whose philosophy on flowers was advocated by those with a background rich in knowledge and understanding of literature and art. Even to intellectuals, such as artists and scholars, something fresh being projected was felt so that many became his supporters, and some even his students.

Ikebana reached the public through magazine articles and lectures on radio, and this extensive journalistic coverage made it popular. It was Adachi Choka, however, who published a correspondence course on ikebana which opened up a way to learn ikebana in a short time. This made it even more available to the general populace.

Japan's invasion of China in 1937 resulted in putting brakes on any modernization of ikebana.

Ikebana Today

What is called modern ikebana is now accepted to cover that period from late 1960s to middle 1980s, now, when experimental work of avant-garde arrangement has passed.

Like postwar avant-garde in other media, ikebana worked together with avant-garde art movements in Western Europe. At first glance there was what could appear to be destruction and denial of traditional ikebana. It was more a form of movement in plastic art, where ideas arose that ikebana should take on the format

Free Style: Camellia / Glass Vase / Sogetsu School, the late Headmaster Teshigahara Sofu

of surrealism. At first, experimental work of having ikebana arrangements stand as objets, "pure works of art," was initiated. Artists composed original works according to their personal natures, creating total abstractions. There were also those who tried to apply principles of automatism, as well as those who were in harmony with artistic ethics of informal art. And we were able to see many ideas and numerous experimentations into new ikebana continued on through the 1960s.

Modern ikebana can rightly date to just after 1970.

Greatly influenced by various modern art movements, and rocked back and forth by various aspects and many kinds of modern art, ikebana started to select out of this profligacy one particular trend. Among artists who had given much thought to the use of objets, were those who started to see hidden forms in traditional folk arts, and began to reassess them. Then, others began to give serious thought to the meaning of individual works of ikebana arrangement and started to ask themselves just what basically the action of creating ikebana meant

Free Style: Cornelian cherry, opsisteris and coleus / Round blue *suiban* / Ohara School, Headmaster Ohara Houn

for mankind.

Avant-garde styles that were prevailing generally until the past decade which could not be distinguished from modern sculpture made of metal, like iron, etc., faded away gradually and plant materials began to be used again. Using plant material does not mean only cut flowers, but refers to stems and branches of trees, driftwood and scrap, which now came to be used as principal material for creating sculptural forms. Those who had asked themselves that searching question of what is ike-bana, now revised their question to ask themselves what relationship there was with nature, and once again started to make sculptural forms using plant materials as main material. Because this use of natural materials looked simply to be return to natural materials, those traditionalists who clung to classical ikebana looked upon this phenomenon as returning to this old ikebana and welcomed it warmly.

However, comparison is necessary with these old concepts which had become established based upon

Free Style: Iris / Yellow container / Ryusei-ha, Headmaster Yoshimura Kasen

consciousness of plants growing in their natural environment, of nature with its four seasons. This new trend was seen to be not just seeking to make ikebana non-representational form, nor seeking expression of these natural abstract basic elements only. Rather we become aware of the fact that people today are concerned with something even more intrinsic: modern man's confrontation with nature. They are trying to understand and express this through their creative work.

Moreover, with a creation such as ikebana whose very being ceases to exist in a short time, and standing so as to be able to clearly affirm this, artists began to develop modern ikebana. And it evolved along lines that ikebana has become "installation," which is to say not merely arrangement, but structure, even though it may be short-lived. But this seeming temporal defect, doesn't it reflect man's own mortality and thus isn't this just what ikebana is about?

In this experimental phase question arose of relationship of ikebana to its environment. Instead of being

Rikka Style: Wintersweet, Japanese apricot (*ume*), pine, camellia, narcissus, small chrysanthemum, spindle tree, boxwood and loquat / Senko rikka vase / Ikenobo, Heasmaster Ikenobo Sen'ei

placed as in the past within confines of domestic living area with its tokonoma alcove, display shelves, tables and furniture, nowadays experiments are being commonly made placing arrangements in galleries or public and commercial spaces, even out-of-doors.

Modern artists started to re-examine reality, groping to establish some organic relationship between nature and ikebana, basing all on their philosphy, which was now ecology. They became deeply conscious that the time had come when man and nature must coexist.

None of this influenced the style of their work directly. But the influence that came from Europe through the work of such as Nash, was vocal in support of the thesis that creation is performance, and the act of creation itself matters most. When this was laid out before Japan's modern artists, they came to accept it, though only relatively recently.

Modern art and modern ikebana both have different roots, but they "cross over" and as phenomenon are looked upon as one and the same, coexisting as such in today's society. Looking at it from an international viewpoint, it may be said to be cross-over of forms between East and West. Conquering the tossing of these kinds of new waves, where new ikebana will go from here is far from certain. We only know that it will continually ask something of nature, and will probably continue making a constructive effort to put man's existence on a firm basis. Only by this will modern ikebana surpass traditional ikebana.

Free Style: Rice stalk, hydrangea, mountain ash, tomato and Japanese anemone / *Tsunodarai* (wooden bucket with two pairs of horns) / Sogetsu School, the late Teshigahara Kasumi

Free Style: Bittersweet, rose mallow and vanda / Ice / Sogetsu School, Headmaster Teshigahara Hiroshi

Rikka Style: Lotus / Rikka vase / Kuwahara Senkei, the late Headmaster Kuwahara Senkei

Seika Style: Cherry blossom and pine / Novel vase / Saga-goryu, Head Teacher Tsujii Hakushu

Seika (Shoka) Style: Cherry blossom / Chinese earthenware container / Seifu Enshu, Headmaster Ashida Ichiba

Seika Style: Cherry blossom / Rectangular bronze basin / Koryu Shohtohkai, Headmistress Ikeda Riei

Free Style: Eucalyptus and rose / Glass vase / Koryu Shooh-kai, Headmaster Semba Riho

Seika Style for *Tanabata* Festival: Bamboo, begonia
evansiana and colored cord / Bronze container /
Shogetsudo Koryu, Headmaster Uematsu Masafusa

Seika Style: Aspidistra / Classical bronze *usubata* container
/ Omuro school, Headmaster Teshima Chitoshi

Free Style: Japanese larch, kerria, fern, skunk cabbage and dried material / Two
rectangular containers / Ohara School, the late Taira Koha

Free Style: Narcissus / Metal container designed by Ito Hosuke / Ohara School, Kudo Kazuhiko

Seika Style: White plum (Japanese apricot) / Three-layered bamboo container / Misho School, Headmaster Hihara Sekiho

Free Style: Japanese iris, thistle and deutzia / Gold-lacquered vessel with lid / Futaba School, Headmaster Horiguchi Gyokuka

Free Style: Painted maple, clematis, elegant lily, caladium and colored wire / Long-necked designer vase / Ishida School, Ishida Shusui

Shoka (Seika) Style: Bittersweet, cosmos and arrowroot / Blue ceramic vase / Ikenobo School, Noda Toho

Free Style: Lilac daphne, lilac and alstroemeria / Novel ceramic container / Misho School, Hihara Toshiki

Free Style: Maple, pampas grass, small chrysanthemum and bupleurum falcatum / Large bowl, *banko* ware, made by Kimura Tahei / Yamato Kado-kai, Headmaster Shimoda Takatoshi

Free Style: Dogwood, Easter lily, vaccinium oldhami and blue delphinium / Glass vase / Sensho Ikenobo, Headmistress Moroizumi Yuyo

Seika Style: Japanese white pine, *ume* (Japanese apricot), camellia, chrysanthemum and narcissus / Bamboo container / Kodo School, Vice-President Mochizuki Nobuhiko

Seika Style: Willow, petrified willow, azalea and gentian / Bronze Enshu container / Enshu School Isshin-kai, Headmaster Mori Isshin

Free Style: Giant reed, maple, cedar, stakes, bamboo gabion, rocks and pebbles / Old waterwheel boards / Chiko School, Headmistress Naruse Kobai

Free Style: Maple, white camellia and smilax China / Round ceramic container / Ikenobo School, Nakamura Muneo

44

Free Style: Pine, anthurium and wisteria vine / Ceramic vase / Koryu Shohtohkai, President Ikeda Masahiro

Free Style: Edgeworthia, nandina and chrysanthemum / Handmade rush vase / Kofu School, Headmistress Yamamoto Saigetsu

Free Style: Japanese apricot (*ume*), cherry blossom, lily magnolia and twenty other kinds of flowers / Acrylic box / Misho School Nakayama Bumpo-kai, Vice-President Nakayama Shoko

Free Style: Lotus / Old Chinese ceramic vase / Seifu
Heika, Vice-President Hayakawa Kenichi

Free Style: Spirea thunbergii, Japanese beauty-berry and
zelkova / Ceramic vase / Ryusei-ha, Yoshimura Takashi

Free Style: Smilax China and rose
petals / Glass vessel / Ichiyo School,
Headmaster Kasuya Akihiro

Free Style: Hydrangea, smilax China and zebra grass / Glass vase / Shinsei School, Headmistress Yamane Yumi

Free Style: Chinese peony, rose, spirea thunbergii, freesia, bellflower, hydrangea leaves and hazel / Container with handle / Ikko School, Headmaster Umeda Hakusen

Free Style: Red pine, narcissus leaves, poppy, stock, carnation and chrysanthemum / No container / Ryusei-ha, Otsubo Kosen

How to Use Flower Holders

In order to make flowers placed into a container even more beautiful, it is important to know how to fix materials when arranging so that they are stable in the container. In ikebana just as much importance is attached to appearance of the base of arrangement as to arrangement itself.

One method of stabilizing flowers into a vase is found in an example at Kanshinji Temple in Kawachi in Osaka. It is a vase and flowers made of gold, silver, copper and iron (A.D. 1330) in which extra short stems are inserted to hold the lotus flower and leaves in place. From this, we can see that techniques to stabilize the materials were applied to offertory flowers before the birth of ikebana.

Offertory flowers in order to express the straight soul (*kokoro*) of those praying are also placed upright. Efforts on getting this to stand upright were made from the time of tatebana and continued on into rikka. With rikka, things were stuffed into the vase, so that the materials stayed up. Rush, straw, cedar leaves and such had been used, but experience showed that bundles of rice straw were more efficient and they came to be used generally.

With seika arrangement, methods of supporting were numerous. The reason for this could be that the base of a seika arrangement should be neat and to keep it orderly, many devices had to be thought up.

Moribana in flat containers and its opposite problem nageire in tall vases made their appearance, and even more techniques came into use.

Supports could be divided into two types: those made only of materials being arranged, or those that are some other supplementary article. These differ with style of ikebana or type of container used. It also depends

Gilt bronze vase
(Kanshinji Temple)

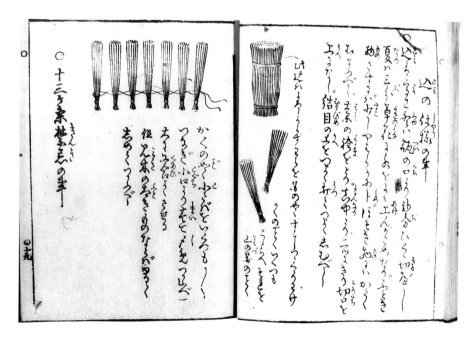

Bundles of Straw

upon what the certain ikebana school prefers. Thus it is that at times, same article or method may be given different names.

For containers that are cylindrical in shape, among techniques of support there is one called *kubari* (distribute). For this method, from one to four pieces of stem of material being used are fixed firmly across the inside mouth of the vase.

Kubari stays are of numerous types. Given names according to shape, such as *ichimonji-kubari* (Japanese ideograph for numeral one), *hangetsu-* (half-moon), *jumonji-* (cross), *choji-* (T-shaped), *suehiro-* (opened folding fan), *kaihari-* (brace) and *ohgi-dome* (folding fan holder).

Among wood used for these supports or braces are Syrian hibiscus, Japanese andromeda, willow, bamboo and cedar.

Another support makes use of Y-shaped branches, or branches split into Y-shape, which are mounted inside

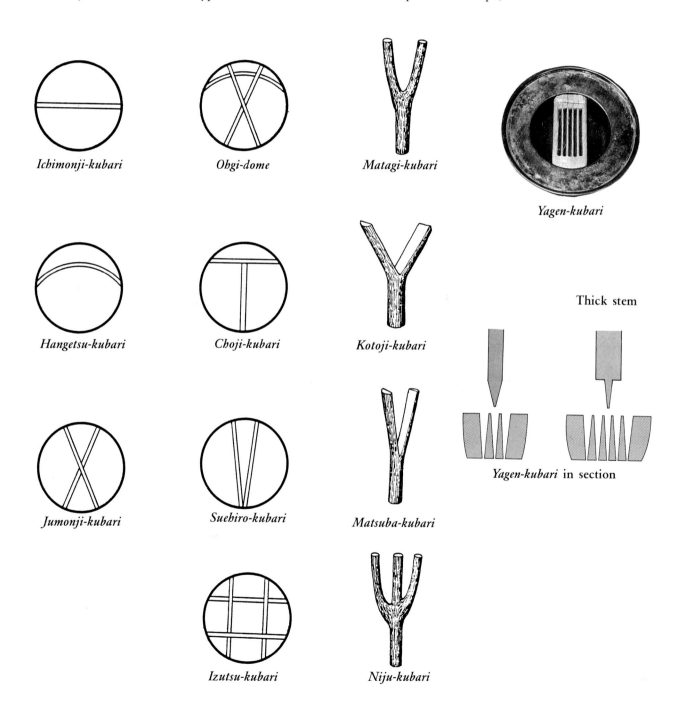

Ichimonji-kubari

Ohgi-dome

Matagi-kubari

Yagen-kubari

Hangetsu-kubari

Choji-kubari

Kotoji-kubari

Thick stem

Jumonji-kubari

Suehiro-kubari

Matsuba-kubari

Yagen-kubari in section

Izutsu-kubari

Niju-kubari

across mouth of vases and used to hold stems in place. These are given such descriptive names as *matsuba-kubari* (pine needle), *matagi-* (forked), *kotoji-* (bridge for strings on *koto*-zither), and *niju-* (double or layered).

A rather special kubari is used in Enshu school called *yagen-kubari* resembling the mortar used to grind herbs into powder. Another resembles the *osa*, reed, part of a weaving loom, and is called *osa-komi*. To make this take a narrow long branch of dracaena and carve thin grooves in it: stems are then inserted into these grooves.

There are other methods for fixing stems into containers as shown in the illustrations.

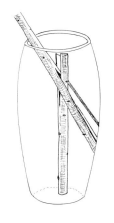 

Soegi-dome (spliced prop)   ***Ichimonji-dome*** (T-shaped prop)

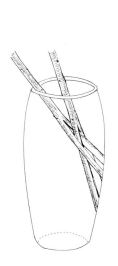   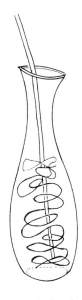

Tatewari-dome (standing prop)   ***Kugiuchi-dome*** (nailed prop)   Spread out after insertion.

Tori-no-su (twisted wire)

 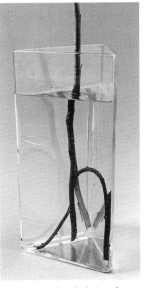  

Toothpick inserted at the end.   A device for helping keep stems upright.   ***Ori-dome*** (bend prop)   ***Jika-dome*** (self-prop)

50

Flower Holders and Stays

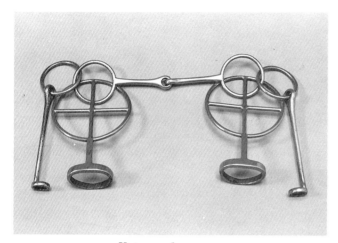

Kutsuwa-dome

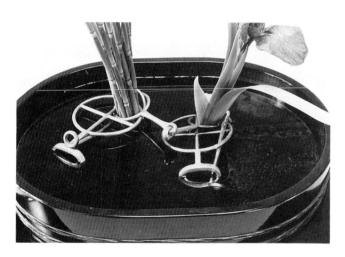

Example of use

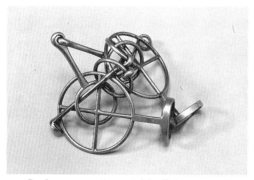

Goshoguruma (imperial bull-drawn cart)

●Flower Holders

For vases with small and medium openings, special contrivances have to be put on either floral materials or containers, discussed fully later. For flat containers like *suiban* and basins for sand arrangements there are numerous ingenious devices, listed below.

As these holders do not rely upon container or support, they must not fall over from weight of flowers, so they must have considerable weight in themselves. Because of this, they are made of copper, iron, lead or stone.

Kame (tortoise)

Mizudori (water bird)

Kani (crab)

●For Seika

Kutsuwa-dome (horse-bit holder): Horse trappings improvised for use as holder, these horse-bits were assembled and used in numerous ways. A wooden horse watering basin was used as container. One flower school had devised 48 different combinations of horse-bits for flower holders, including crab, lobster, water fowl, tortoise and imperial cart.

Gotoku-dome (tripod holder): Tripod used in a *hibachi*, over a fire upon which an iron kettle or pot was placed. The tripod was used as flower holder, and at

Kudari-gani (descending crab)

Nobori-gani (climbing crab)

Gotoku-dome (tripod)

Kame-dome (tortoise)

Jakago-dome (gabion)

Example

Kanzemizu-dome (whirlpool)

Shippo

Kenzan

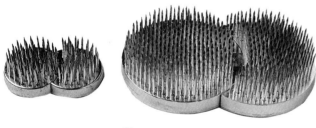

Kenzan

Kenzan

times, two or three were placed one within another, to form a larger holder. This was placed in the container and was ideal for material with large stems such as large branches.

Kani-dome (crab holder): This metal crab-shaped stand was used in tea ceremony, upon which the lid of the iron tea kettle was placed lest it damage *tatami*. Stems of floral material were inserted between claws and legs or between two legs. There were even different techniques in their use and were designated as *nobori-gani* (ascending crab) and *kudari-gani* (descending crab) method of arrangement.

Kame-dome (tortoise holder): Into the hexagonal design of tortoise shell, holes were cut, into which stems of materials were inserted. When any stem did not fill its hole, additional short stems were inserted, or the stem was broken and bent up to stabilize it.

Jakago-dome (gabion holder): Wire-mesh tubular-shaped basket holding small pebbles as ballast.

Kanzesui-dome (whirlpool holder): Swirling water was the motif for this holder. It is used in the same way as tortoise holder.

Shippo (shippo holder): This circular pattern is often found in family crests and has been copied from it. There is the single circle one, as well as those with two circles interlocked, and three circles interlocked. There are schools of ikebana which use these for moribana and free-style arrangement.

●For Moribana and Free-style Arrangement

Kenzan (needle holder): When moribana was devised, stays and props used for seika arrangement were generally taken over, but after kenzan needle holder was introduced, it was only a matter of time before this easy-to-use holder spread quickly. At present it is even used for seika. In different schools of ikebana, each has made its own innovations, such as combining kenzan with tortoise shell holder or shippo holder, and even wooden Y-bar has been attached atop kenzan. Flower holders themselves were made to be part of the arrangement at base of stems, but kenzan is only to hold stem in place. When kenzan is used, arrangement should be so made that it will not show; another method is to cover it with small pebbles.

Technique of Training Branches

In ikebana there is a technique called *tameru* by which stems and branches can be given more graceful shape by bending. The purpose of doing this is to improve a special characteristic of the material or to express more clearly the floral style, or to help carry out the design and intention of the composition.

To be able to carry out the bending properly, it becomes necessary to know the basic character of the material as well as its special characteristic. For example, some branches are not resilient and being brittle will break when bending is tried. To bend and train stems successfully there are many techniques and each of them differs according to inherent character of the material.

●Treatment for Branch Material

Application of Wedges: Technique most often used with seika to give desired beautiful curve to branch material. At the point where curve is desired, take small saw and make cut on side that will be outer side of curve. Then V-shaped wedge, usually made from the same branch material is inserted into cut.

Notching: On outer side of the desired curve, make

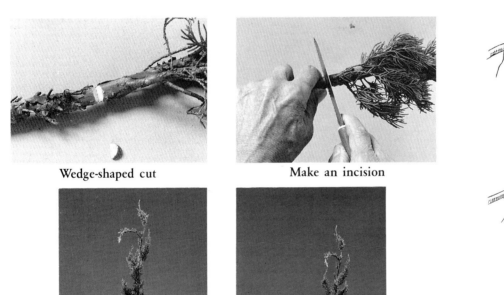

Wedge-shaped cut

Make an incision

Before bending

Bent with wedges inserted

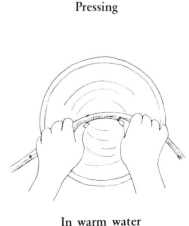

With a wedge

Pressing

In warm water

54

a notch using flower scissors. Then hold branch with both hands, one on either side of cut, thumbs underside, and pull downwards to get desired curve.

Bending: If branch or stem is slimmer and responds to bending without putting notch into it, then desired curve should be made by holding branch with two hands and again placing two thumbs underside of branch, and bending using pressure on thumbs.

Twisting: In this twisting method the palm of one hand is placed above and the other underneath the branch to begin with and then the material is gently twisted (hand position is similar to wringing out towels). In twisting, fibrous tissues of the stem are broken down so that the desired curve may be acquired.

Among others are techniques of grasping and kneading, of pushing, and of heating up and soaking in warm water.

●Treatment of Flower Material

Stroking: Used with leaf material and those materials with stems that are hollow. One way is to twist leaf around your finger, another by holding leaf or stem and drawing it between thumb and forefinger of other hand and stroking or rubbing lightly with thumb.

Crushing: Used on stems of flowers. With fingers or fingernails and even handles of scissors, crush gently and bend to shape.

Pinning: Used in seika arrangement when flowers such as chrysanthemum are given an extreme curve. First curve floral stem to desired curve, and to keep it from springing back up, take drill and make hole, then pass bamboo stick through it as though pinning it.

Among other techniques, there is one for flower stems that are hollow. In this, a metal wire is inserted into the stem and then curved to shape.

Crushing

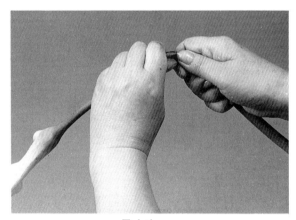

Twisting

Stroking

Using a wire

Various Containers

Containers are for the purpose of holding an ikebana arrangement. Thus they differ with style of arrangement, as well as with period in which these arrangements were made.

At the time of early tatebana when it was one of three utensils displayed in the alcove, either *tobyoshi-guchi* vase (with flared out rim, which narrows down) or *momozoko* (slim neck with round peach-like base) were used. However, one is overwhelmed by many different kinds of containers found among those drawn in *Tatebana Zukan* (Tatebana Illustrated).

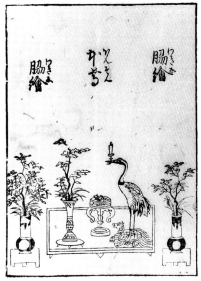

Mitsugusoku

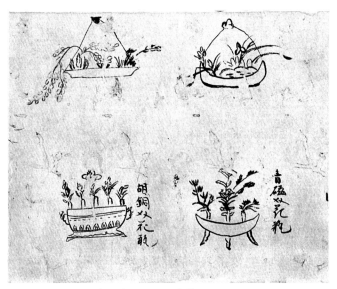

Early records of vases and flower arrangements

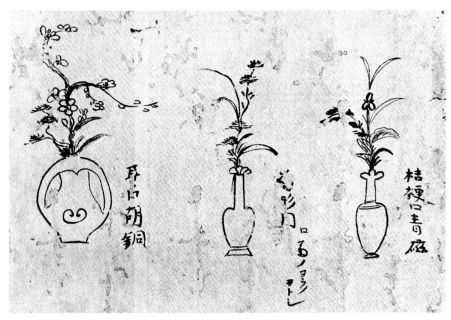

From *Tatebana Zukan* (Illustrations of Tatebana Arrangements)
Property of Yomei Bunko, Kyoto.

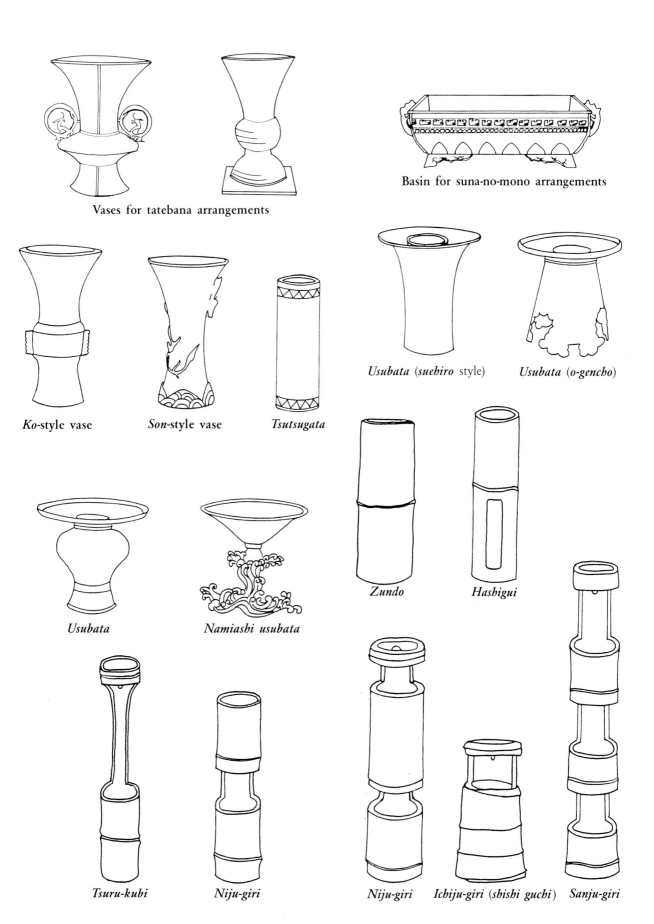

Vases for tatebana arrangements

Basin for suna-no-mono arrangements

Ko-style vase   *Son*-style vase   *Tsutsugata*

Usubata (*suehiro* style)   *Usubata* (*o-gencho*)

Usubata   *Namiashi usubata*

Zundo   *Hashigui*

Tsuru-kubi   *Niju-giri*

Niju-giri   *Ichiju-giri* (*shishi guchi*)   *Sanju-giri*

At about this same time, boat-shaped hanging containers appear in great numbers. In this technique, flowers appear to be moving in a breeze. This is an arrangement and container of the early period of nageire.

Having started out as one of three utensils placed in tokonoma, many of these vases for tatebana have wide rims and are trim in shape. Since tatebana itself is rather voluminous, they have rims that flare out, tapering down into a trim middle area and then widening out at base to appear solid and stable, giving exceptional balance to the entire arrangement.

Rikka in *suna-no-mono* (containers with sand) were made in flat basins, which at that time were mostly metal containers of bronzes of various alloys, as well as some of celadon, most of these imported from China.

Seika arrangements usually made use of the same containers as were used for tatebana. Bronze receptacle called *usubata* is most representative for seika. Having a large flat circular and extremely shallow rim crowning its upper portion, it appeared somewhat like a folding fan and was also known as *suehiro* (folding fan opened

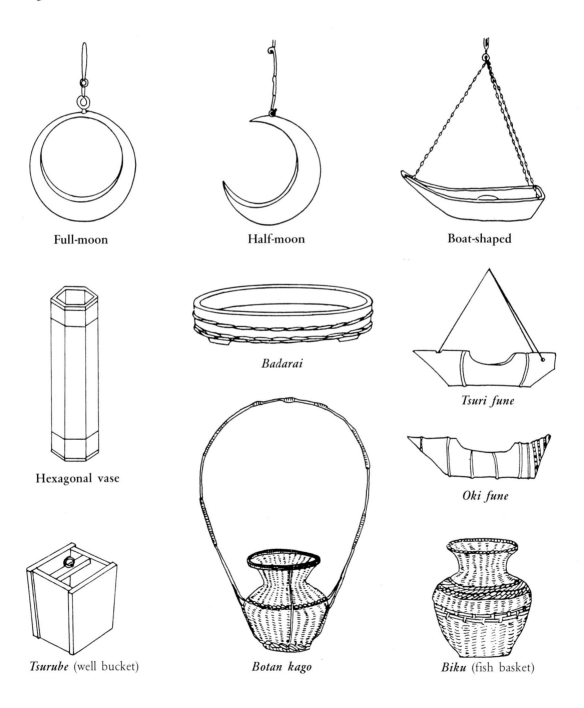

Full-moon

Half-moon

Boat-shaped

Badarai

Hexagonal vase

Tsuri fune

Oki fune

Tsurube (well bucket)

Botan kago

Biku (fish basket)

out). Its lower half or base usually varied, but those with legs in shape of waves, monkeys, tortoises were used exclusively by Enshu school and came to be known as Enshu *usubata*.

Other metal containers included those in shapes of wine casks, wine bottles, cylinders, moons (full- and crescent-), and boats, as well as flat *suiban* containers.

Containers made from bamboo are best known by those tall cylinders, some being plain cylinder with flowers inserted into top joint, others with extra opening in the next joint down, as well as boat-shaped ones, and each with unlimited variations. These same shapes have been reproduced in wood, lacquerware and ceramic.

Moribana was a style created after Meiji Restoration when influences from Europe and America were taking hold. Drawn by colorfulness of Western flowers, flowers were "piled" into a container. *Suiban* flat containers came to be associated with moribana. A variety of shapes are found, such as pedestalled compote dish, and those almost always ceramic.

Free-style arrangement uses same containers as nage-ire, heika, moribana.

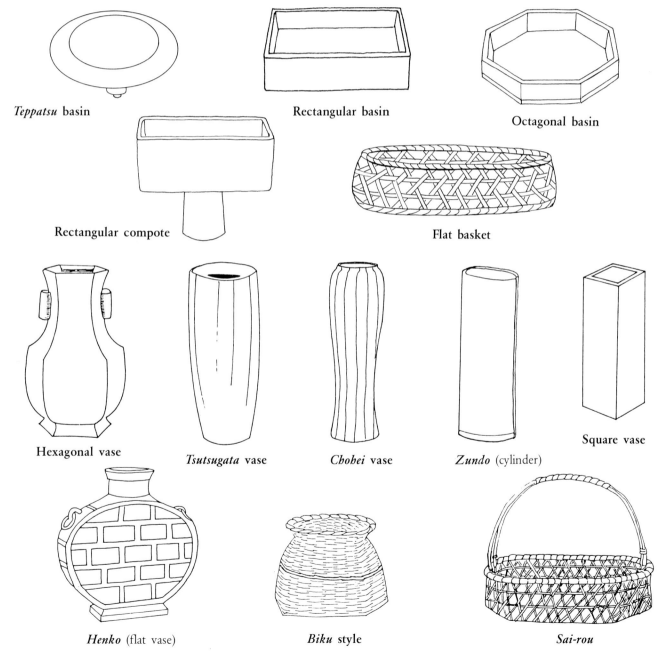

Teppatsu basin

Rectangular basin

Octagonal basin

Rectangular compote

Flat basket

Hexagonal vase

Tsutsugata vase

Chohei vase

Zundo (cylinder)

Square vase

Henko (flat vase)

Biku style

Sai-rou

CHRONOLOGICAL TABLE OF HISTORY OF IKEBANA

Period	General Trend	Main events
B.C. 2000		Jomon, Neolithic Period
500 A.D.....		Yayoi, Late Neolithic Period
250		From about this period religious belief held that deity descends to earth through trees, boulders, waterfalls
350		Unification of Yamato Imperial state in Osaka-Nara area (Yamato Plain)
538		Introduction of Buddhism
607		Horyuji, first Buddhist temple, built near Nara
710	PRE-IKEBANA	Capital transferred to Heijo-Nara
759		*Manyoshu*, Japan's oldest anthology of poems, compiled. Includes numerous poems mentioning flowers
794		Capital moves to Heian-Kyoto Beginning of palace-style architecture
810		Offertory flowers to deity and Buddha organized by priest at Gango-ji Temple, Nara
864	FLOWERS START BEING PLACED IN A VESSEL	Cherry-viewing party held by Emperor Seiwa in Kyoto
905		Phrase "to arrange flowers" appears in literature
913		From this time on, competitions for best chrysanthemums, flowering trees and gardens were frequently held at Court in Kyoto
1000		*Pillow Book* mentions placing cherry blossoms in celadon vase in imperial garden
1012		*Tale of Genji* mentions similar activity
1066		*Magna Carta*
1150		*Angkor Wat built*
1271		*Marco Polo starts trip to East*
1298		Offertory flowers appear incised on "itabi" tomb stones or tablets
1309		Picture scrolls show offertory flowers, bonsai and arranging of flowers

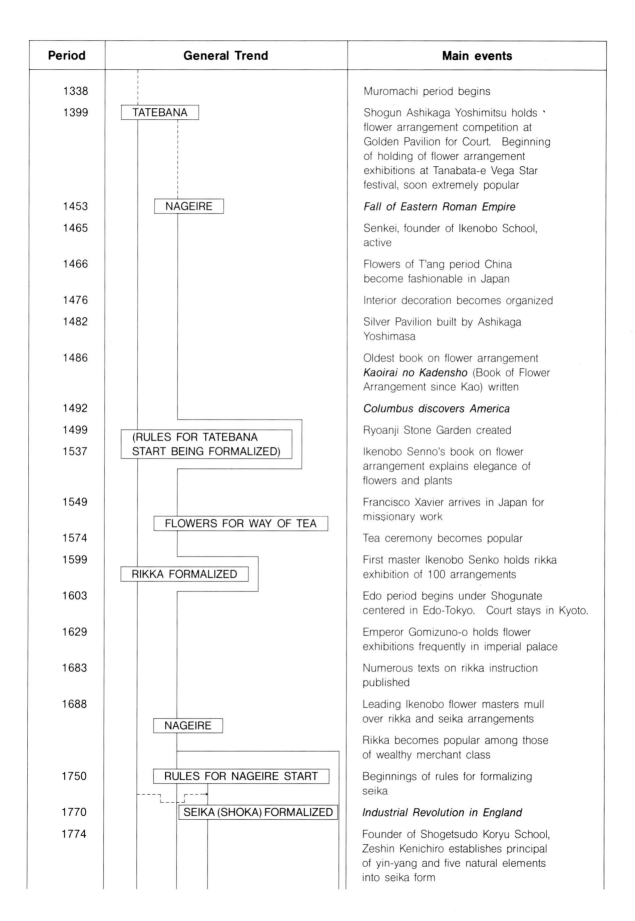

Period	General Trend	Main events
1338		Muromachi period begins
1399	TATEBANA	Shogun Ashikaga Yoshimitsu holds flower arrangement competition at Golden Pavilion for Court. Beginning of holding of flower arrangement exhibitions at Tanabata-e Vega Star festival, soon extremely popular
1453	NAGEIRE	*Fall of Eastern Roman Empire*
1465		Senkei, founder of Ikenobo School, active
1466		Flowers of T'ang period China become fashionable in Japan
1476		Interior decoration becomes organized
1482		Silver Pavilion built by Ashikaga Yoshimasa
1486		Oldest book on flower arrangement *Kaoirai no Kadensho* (Book of Flower Arrangement since Kao) written
1492		*Columbus discovers America*
1499	(RULES FOR TATEBANA START BEING FORMALIZED)	Ryoanji Stone Garden created
1537		Ikenobo Senno's book on flower arrangement explains elegance of flowers and plants
1549	FLOWERS FOR WAY OF TEA	Francisco Xavier arrives in Japan for missionary work
1574		Tea ceremony becomes popular
1599	RIKKA FORMALIZED	First master Ikenobo Senko holds rikka exhibition of 100 arrangements
1603		Edo period begins under Shogunate centered in Edo-Tokyo. Court stays in Kyoto.
1629		Emperor Gomizuno-o holds flower exhibitions frequently in imperial palace
1683		Numerous texts on rikka instruction published
1688	NAGEIRE	Leading Ikenobo flower masters mull over rikka and seika arrangements
		Rikka becomes popular among those of wealthy merchant class
1750	RULES FOR NAGEIRE START	Beginnings of rules for formalizing seika
1770	SEIKA (SHOKA) FORMALIZED	*Industrial Revolution in England*
1774		Founder of Shogetsudo Koryu School, Zeshin Kenichiro establishes principal of yin-yang and five natural elements into seika form

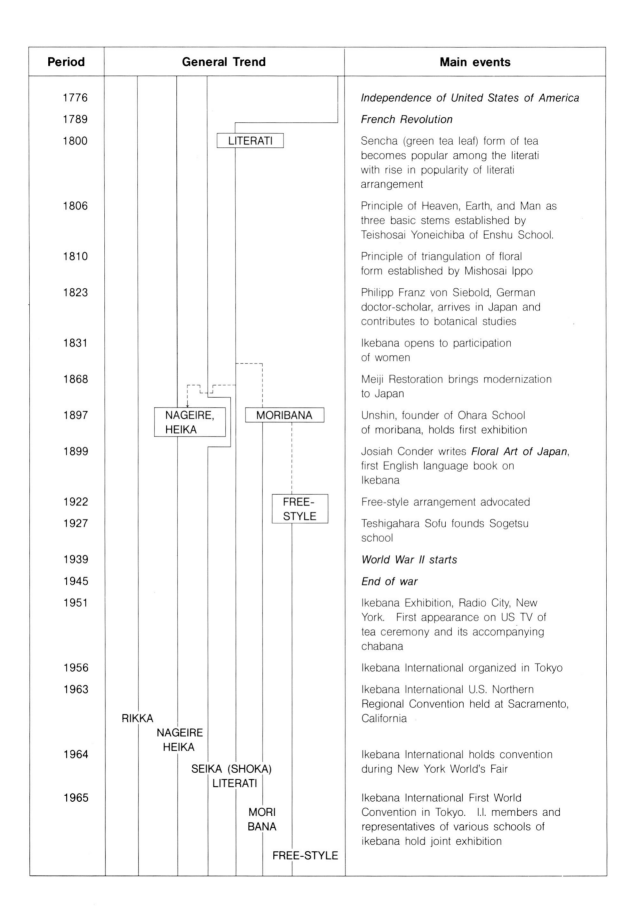

Period	General Trend				Main events
1776					*Independence of United States of America*
1789					*French Revolution*
1800			LITERATI		Sencha (green tea leaf) form of tea becomes popular among the literati with rise in popularity of literati arrangement
1806					Principle of Heaven, Earth, and Man as three basic stems established by Teishosai Yoneichiba of Enshu School.
1810					Principle of triangulation of floral form established by Mishosai Ippo
1823					Philipp Franz von Siebold, German doctor-scholar, arrives in Japan and contributes to botanical studies
1831					Ikebana opens to participation of women
1868					Meiji Restoration brings modernization to Japan
1897		NAGEIRE, HEIKA		MORIBANA	Unshin, founder of Ohara School of moribana, holds first exhibition
1899					Josiah Conder writes *Floral Art of Japan*, first English language book on Ikebana
1922				FREE-STYLE	Free-style arrangement advocated
1927					Teshigahara Sofu founds Sogetsu school
1939					*World War II starts*
1945					*End of war*
1951					Ikebana Exhibition, Radio City, New York. First appearance on US TV of tea ceremony and its accompanying chabana
1956					Ikebana International organized in Tokyo
1963	RIKKA NAGEIRE HEIKA				Ikebana International U.S. Northern Regional Convention held at Sacramento, California
1964		SEIKA (SHOKA) LITERATI			Ikebana International holds convention during New York World's Fair
1965			MORI BANA	FREE-STYLE	Ikebana International First World Convention in Tokyo. I.I. members and representatives of various schools of ikebana hold joint exhibition

Index

Adachi Choka, 32
Ashikaga Yoshimitsu, 13
badarai, 58
biku, 58, 59
boat-shaped vase, 58
Bokie Kotoba, 15
bonkei, 12
botan kago, 58
bunjin-bana, 28, 29
bunjin-ike, 32
cha-do, 6
chabana, 6, 22
chanoyu-no-hana, 22
chi (earth), 27
Chiba Ryuboku, 26
chohei vase, 59
choji-kubari, 49
Choju Giga, 10
Daijuin Ishin, 21
doboshu, 15
dogu, 20
dojo, 19
Doku school, 26, 27
Enshu school, 26, 27
flat basket, 59
Floral Art of Japan, 30
full-moon vase, 58
Genji school, 26
gilt-bronze lotus, 10
Gomizuno-o, 6, 19
goshoguruma, 51
gotoku-dome, 52
gyo, 17, 24
half-moon vase, 58
hana-awase, 6, 12, 14
Hanafu, 13
hangetsu-kubari, 49
hashigui, 57
henko, 59
hexagonal vase, 58, 59
hibachi, 48
History of Vases, 29
hongatte-no-hana, 16
ichiju-giri, 57
ichimonji-dome, 50
ichimonji-kubari, 49
iemoto, 26
Ikai Sanzaemon, 21

ikebana, 6, 8
Ikenobo Sen'ei, 17
Ikenobo Senjun Kadensho, 17
Ikenobo Senko, 18
Ikenobo Senno, 16
Ikenobo Senoh, 20
Imai Isshikensofu, 26, 27
Inoue Tomosada, 24
Irie school, 26, 27
izutsu-kubari, 49
jakago-dome, 52, 53
jika-dome, 50
jin (man), 27
Josiah Conder, 30
Juichiya Taemon, 21
jumonji-kubari, 49
kadomatsu, 10, 11
kaihari-kubari, 49
kame, 51
kame-dome, 52, 53
kani, 51
kani-dome, 53
Kanmon-gyoki, 13
kanzemizu-dome, 52
Kaoirai no Kadensho, 12
Kasuga Gongen Reigenki Emaki, 14
Katsura Rikyu, 8
kazari-dana, 14
kenzan, 53
kiku-awase, 12
Kinkakuji Temple, 12
Kodo school, 27
Kokin-waka-shu, 12
Koryu school, 26, 27
ko-style vase, 57
kotoji-kubari, 49
kubari, 49
kudari-gani, 52
kugiuchi-dome, 50
Kundaikan Sochoki, 14
kutsuwa-dome, 51, 52
Kuwahara Fushunken Senkei, 21
Kyofu school, 32
laurilignosa culture, 8
literati arrangement, 7, 28, 29
Makura-no-soshi, 12
Manyoshu, 11
matagi-kubari, 49, 50

matsuba-kubari, 50
minakuchi, 11
Misho school, 27
mitsugusoku, 56
mizudori, 51
momozoko, 56
Mon'ami, 15
Mon'ami Kadensho, 13
mono-awase, 13
moribana, 7, 30
nageire, 6, 16
nageire-hana, 22
namiashi usubata, 57
niju-giri, 57
niju-kubari, 49
Ninety-Three Rikka Arrangement, 18
Noami, 15
nobori-gani, 52
octagonal basin, 59
Ohara school, 30
Ohara Unshin, 30
Ohi Minobu, 5
ohgi-dome, 49
oki fune, 58
ori-dome, 50
osa-komi, 50
oshi-ita, 14
Rakubodo Gyozan, 24
rectangular basin, 59
rectangular compote, 59
renga, 19
rikka, 6, 16
Rikka Jisei Sho, 16
Ryuami, 15
sa-do, 13
Saegusa Festival, 11
sai-rou, 59
Sakyamuni, 16
sanju-giri, 57
seika, 24
sencha, 29
Sen'ei Densho, 17
Sen-no-Rikyu, 22
Sendensho, 16
Senko II, 6, 19, 20
Senno Kuden, 17
senzai-awase, 12
Shaka, 16

shichiseki horaku-no-hana, 12
Shigemori Mirei, 5
shin, 17, 20, 24
shin-no-hana, 16
shippo, 53
Shofu school, 26, 27
Shogetsudo Koryu, 27
shoin, 14
shoin-zukuri, 14
shoji, 14
shoka, 24
Shugakuin Rikyu, 9
Shuhan Ron, 14
Shunjuken Ichiyo, 26
so, 17, 24
Soami, 15
soegi-dome, 50
son-style vase, 57
Sosei Kadenoho, 13
square vase, 59

suehiro, 58
suehiro-kubari, 49
suiban, 30, 51
sukiya, 7, 23
suna-no-mono, 12, 58
Takada Anryubo Shugyoku, 21
Tanabata Vega-star Festival, 12
tamagushi, 10
tameru, 54
tatami, 14
tatebana, 6, 13, 16, 22
Tatebana Zukan, 56
tatewari-dome, 50
ten (heaven), 27
teppatsu basin, 59
Teshigahara Sofu, 32
tobyoshi-guchi vase, 56
Tofuku Kadan, 24
Tsuri fune, 58
tokonoma, 14

tori-no-su, 50
Toyotomi Hideyoshi, 18
tsuchibyoshi-guchi vase, 56
tsurube, 58
tsuru-kuchi, 57
tsutsugata vase, 57, 59
usubata, 57, 58
uta-awase, 13
yagen-kubari, 49, 50
Yamane Suido, 32
Yamane Yuzo, 5
yang, 27
yin, 27
yorishiro, 6, 10
Yúan Hung-tao, 29
zashiki, 6
zashiki drawing room, 14
zundo, 57